DECODING
MAORI
COSMOLOGY

"*Decoding Maori Cosmology* is sure to be controversial. Its major premise claims that an archaic, matriarchal tradition, or great Mother Goddess culture, gave birth to parallel mythological systems all across the globe after 10,000 BCE. Continuing his series that researches the evidence for cultural diffusion, Laird Scranton uses comparative linguistics as well as corresponding cosmologies, concepts, architectures, and artifacts in order to link the Maori of New Zealand with Gobekli Tepe in Turkey, the Sakti Cult of Tamil India, dynastic and predynastic Egypt, Skara Brae in Northern Scotland, the Dogon tribe of Mali, and the Buddhism of Tibet and elsewhere. In addition, he clearly and skillfully demonstrates how these diverse peoples of long ago fully understood the fundamental principles of quantum physics and string theory. This book is an essential piece of the puzzle showing the true picture of our ancient past."

GARY A. DAVID, AUTHOR OF
JOURNEY OF THE SERPENT PEOPLE:
HOPI MIGRATIONS AND STAR CORRELATIONS

"With every book Laird Scranton writes, he take us deeper into understanding our origin and ourselves. Using his solid foundation of Dogon, Egyptian, Chinese, and Scottish cultures he again displays to the reader the complexities inherent in ancient civilizations and provides additional insights into our obscured past. Laird continues to broaden our understanding of the advanced technical concepts that are fundamental to world myths, concepts so advanced that we are only rediscovering many of them today. He suggests that there is an archaic connection between these diverse cultures, with the ancient cosmology of the Maori of New Zealand further validating this interconnected web of language, culture, science, and tradition. *Decoding Maori Cosmology* presents intriguing correlations and compelling arguments that cause you to stop and think."

RITA LOUISE, PH.D., COAUTHOR OF
*THE E.T. CHRONICLES: WHAT MYTHS AND LEGENDS
TELL US ABOUT HUMAN ORIGINS*

DECODING MAORI COSMOLOGY

The Ancient Origins of New Zealand's Indigenous Culture

LAIRD SCRANTON

Inner Traditions
Rochester, Vermont

Inner Traditions
One Park Street
Rochester, Vermont 05767
www.InnerTraditions.com

Text stock is SFI certified

Library of Congress Cataloging-in-Publication Data
Names: Scranton, Laird, 1953– author.
Title: Decoding Maori cosmology : the ancient origins of New Zealand's
    indigenous culture / Laird Scranton.
Description: Rochester, Vermont : Inner Traditions, 2018. | Includes
    bibliographical references and index.
Identifiers: LCCN 2017039611 (print) | LCCN 2017042546 (e-book) |
    ISBN 9781620557051 (paperback) | ISBN 9781620557068 (e-book)
Subjects: LCSH: Cosmology, Maori. | Mythology, Maori. | Maori (New Zealand
    people)—Folklore. | Creation—Mythology. | Mythology—Comparative studies. |
    BISAC: BODY, MIND & SPIRIT / Mythical Civilizations. | SOCIAL SCIENCE /
    Anthropology / Cultural. | BODY, MIND & SPIRIT / Unexplained Phenomena.
Classification: LCC DU423.C63 S37 2018 (print) | LCC DU423.C63 (e-book) |
    DDC 299/.92442—dc23
LC record available at https://lccn.loc.gov/2017039611

Printed and bound in the United States by Lake Book Manufacturing, Inc.
The text stock is SFI certified. The Sustainable Forestry Initiative® program promotes
sustainable forest management.

10 9 8 7 6 5 4 3 2 1

Text design by Virginia Scott Bowman and layout by Priscilla Baker

This book was typeset in Garamond Premier Pro with Benguiat, Churchward Maori, and
Arquitecta used as display typefaces

The image on page 114 appears courtesy of its creator through Creative Commons,
https://creativecommons.org/licenses/by-sa/2.0/legalcode

To send correspondence to the author of this book, mail a first-class letter to the author c/o
Inner Traditions • Bear & Company, One Park Street, Rochester, VT 05767, and we will
forward the communication, or contact the author directly at **scrantonlr@aol.com**.

Contents

Acknowledgments   vii

1   Introduction to the Maori   1

2   Historical Overview of the Esoteric Tradition   10

3   Deities of the Maori Pantheon   19

4   Parallels to Dogon Cosmology   31

5   Mythic Themes of Maori Cosmology   45

6   Pre-Buddhist and Hindu Influences on
Maori Religion   52

7   Echoes of Gobekli Tepe among the Maori   58

8   Maori and Tamil Word Correlations   65

9   Evidence of the Sakti Cult in Maori Culture   71

10   Symbolic Aspects of Ganesha in Maori Cosmology   75

11   Ancient Egyptian Word Correlations to the Maori   81

12 Yah and Maori Concepts of Creation from Light   87

13 Foundational Philosophies in Maori Cosmology   95

14 Maori References to the Field of Arou   101

15 The Wharekura, or School of Reeds   111

16 Maori Concepts of the Priesthood and
Sacred Spots   119

17 Maori Myth of the Overturning of the Earth Mother   124

18 Tracks of the Peti and the Papae in New Zealand   131

19 Symbolism of the Seven Mythic Canoes
of the Maori   140

20 The Sacrifice of the Nummo   144

21 Putting the Maori References in Context   150

Notes   163

Bibliography   176

Index   179

Acknowledgments

It goes without saying that this volume owes a debt of thanks to my sister, Lizzy Thoresen, who reached out into the world to make New Zealand her home and has long championed its beauty, the sensibilities of its people, and its greater significance in the world. I would also like to acknowledge my nephew, Rafael Arenos, who has always connected with my interests and steadfastly supported my efforts. Thanks are due again to my wife and best friend, Risa, my son, Isaac, and my daughter, Hannah, who each bring their own significant influences to the work that I do and allow me to use them as sounding boards for each new obscure nuance of my research. I would like to thank John Anthony West, who continues to be an avid promoter of my work, even when it may skirt the fringes of his own well-formed outlooks. In particular, I would like to thank the many people who take the time to read my books, attend my presentations, and otherwise introduce themselves into my life.

1 Introduction to the Maori

I initially undertook to write this book in the summer of 2003, shortly after having self-published *Hidden Meanings: A Study of the Founding Symbols of Civilization* (later republished by Inner Traditions as *The Science of the Dogon*). The manuscript for *Hidden Meanings* had begun simply as an organized set of working notes that I had kept for my Dogon studies. Over time, these notes grew in length to the point where they approximated a book, and so I made the decision to self-publish them. During this same period of self-study, I had acquired a copy of New Zealand ethnographer Elsdon Best's *Maori Religion and Mythology,* had noticed similarities between the Dogon and Maori cosmologies, and had been reading it for comparison to the Dogon. Although outwardly the Dogon and the Maori are distant cultures with no obvious links of heritage (one located in Northwest Africa and the other in Polynesia), I could see that the Maori concept of the *po* as an atom-like component of matter was a match for the similar Dogon concept. Likewise, details of the Maori esoteric tradition and how it was passed down from generation to generation were quite similar to the Dogon tradition. These practices implied that, despite the great distance between cultures, the symbology of this tribal culture from New Zealand must have arisen out of a system of cosmology that was substantially similar to that of the Dogon.

By this early point in my studies, I already understood that language could be a key to correlating ancient concepts between cultures, so I did a cursory review of a Maori-English dictionary to test the limits of possible correspondence. The dictionary revealed certain areas of linguistic overlap, but it also reflected significant differences in word forms that I was not yet competent to explain. Year after year, as each new book in my series on ancient cosmology was brought to completion, it again became my intention to take up these studies and develop a book about Maori cosmology. But inevitably, some logical next phase in my comparative work from Africa to Egypt, India, Tibet, and China would assert itself and convince me to set the Maori project aside, with hopes of continuing it at some future date.

More than a decade later, I now look on these delays in process as having been fortuitous ones. Each project that pushed its way ahead of the Maori book brought with it a degree of familiarity with yet another era of ancient cosmology that I now see as having direct bearing on the Maori tradition. Moreover, each cosmological era was characterized by certain key terms and mythic themes drawn from its own related language.

For example, I believe that insights into the archaic era of Gobekli Tepe can often be found in Turkish word forms. The matriarchal era of the Sakti Cult is perhaps best reflected in Tamil roots of the Dravidian languages in southern India. The Vedic, Buddhist, and Hindu eras express themselves in Sanskrit. Terms of the Neolithic era of the cosmology can be recognized through comparison to words of the Faroese, Icelandic, and Scottish-Gaelic languages. Similarly, the Dogon era of the cosmology came into focus for me through the correlation of Dogon words and ancient Egyptian hieroglyphic words, which often take the same form as Hebrew words. The Maori system of cosmology, which is rooted in a relatively recent historical period, is couched in a language that seems to be an effective clearinghouse for the cosmological words of each of these prior eras. To find these words commingled within the Maori language implies that each era is likely to have had an ancestral influence on the Maori tradition.

For those who may not be familiar with regions in Polynesia, New Zealand is a spectacularly scenic island country in the southwestern Pacific Ocean, situated to the southeast of Thailand and just east of the continent of Australia. It consists of two main landmasses, known as the North Island and the South Island, along with a number of other smaller islands. Because of its remote location, New Zealand was one of the last lands on our planet known to be permanently occupied by people. The Maori ("maow-ree") are a native tribal group of New Zealand and are considered by many to have been the original inhabitants of these beautiful islands. Maori tribal groups were found to be living in New Zealand when European explorers first arrived. In 1642 the Dutch explorer Abel Tasman became the first European explorer to happen upon New Zealand, at which time he reported finding a population of nearly one hundred thousand Maori residing there, located primarily in the northern regions of the North Island. In 1769 the English sea captain James Cook landed in New Zealand and made the first efforts to map the islands. It was not until 1814 that Christian missionaries arrived in New Zealand and attempted to convert the native population to Christianity. Although the Maori culture rested on many of its societal advancements, these missionaries also brought outside education and skills of literacy to the natives, along with instruction in techniques of agriculture.

Tradition holds that the Maori felt no need to identify themselves by a collective name until the Europeans arrived. At that time they adopted the name *Maori*, a term that means "native" or "indigenous." In the words of their native language, the Maori refer to themselves generically as the *tangata whenua*, the "human beings of the earth," or indigenous people of New Zealand. Although they are traditionally understood to have been the first group to populate the islands, the Maori are thought to have migrated to New Zealand by canoe in comparatively recent times, less than a thousand years ago (circa 1200 CE), from a mythical homeland in eastern Polynesia called Hawaiki. An official government website in New Zealand states, "New Zealand has a shorter human history than any other country. The precise date of settlement is a matter of debate, but current understanding is that the first arrivals came from East Polynesia in the 13th century. It was not until 1642 that Europeans became aware the country existed."[1]

One knowledgeable commentator, a New Zealand public servant and scholar named Edward Tregear, took exception with the conventional timeline for the arrival of the Maori in New Zealand, arguing that there is evidence to suggest that Maori settlement on the islands must have occurred at a much earlier date. Tregear, who lived and wrote in the late 1800s and early 1900s, devoted much study to the history of the Maori, to comparative Polynesian linguistics, and to the Maori language. These studies led Tregear to compile an authoritative dictionary of their language, as well as to author other books about Maori history and culture. Tregear writes in his 1885 book *The Aryan Maori*, "If [Maori] genealogies are to be trusted, the canoes bringing them [to New Zealand] arrived only two or three hundred years ago. I believe that those who have studied the subject most are unanimous in declaring that the Maoris have been in New Zealand very much longer; that, from the very extensive cultivations, fortifications, etc., New Zealand gives evidence [to this fact].[2]

From the beginning, the Maori are understood to have relied primarily on hunting and gathering for their subsistence, but they are also known to have cultivated gardens and to have fished and made use of other bounty from the sea that surrounds the islands of New Zealand. From these resources, the Maori are thought to have developed a good standard of living, although a comparatively lower one than that of the Europeans who made their arrival in the 1600s.

Because the Maori are genetically Polynesian, the roots of their culture and language are also distinctly Polynesian and so bear a close resemblance to those of other Polynesian peoples. From a linguistic perspective, Tregear's comparative Maori-Polynesian dictionary amply shows this to be the case. But since the Maori lived for several centuries in relative isolation from the outside world, their outlook on important concepts of cosmology may have also been better sheltered from outside influences and so might possibly be more reflective of ancient forms than the outlooks of people from other Polynesian cultures. In the seventeenth century, the arrival of the first Europeans in New Zealand brought the threat of religious assimilation and loss of cultural identity for many of the Maori people, along with problems that have continued into modern times. According to a 2013 census, the tribal culture consists of nearly six hundred thousand individuals and represents perhaps 15 percent of the current population of New Zealand. More than an additional one hundred thousand Maori also live in nearby Australia.

Despite the seemingly recent date of their culture, in the eyes of a comparative cosmologist such as myself, the Maori are the keepers of a creation tradition that offers many outward points of comparison to cultures from other widespread regions of the world that are demonstrably much more ancient. Even a cursory familiarity with the Maori language reveals words whose form and usage bear overt similarities to the names of significant deities and concepts of classic ancient creation traditions. From that perspective, the Maori might be seen as a largely untapped source of potentially useful information about the meanings of ancient cosmological words, symbols, concepts, and practices. Likewise, their history might provide important clues as to how the ancient cosmological tradition that we have been pursuing may have spread during historical times.

This book is the seventh in a series of volumes whose focus is on ancient cosmology and language. One goal of the series is to broaden our understanding of the outwardly similar practices of various ancient classical creation traditions through the use of various comparative techniques. Previous volumes of this series have been dedicated to the cosmologies of the Dogon (pronounced "Dough-gun") tribe of Mali in Africa, the myths and symbols of ancient Egypt, the practices of Buddhism, the cosmology and language of a priestly Tibetan tribe called the Na-Khi, and the earliest creation traditions of ancient China. We have offered perspectives through which each of these traditions might be traced from an archaic source, evidence of whose influence was first seen at Gobekli Tepe in the region of the Fertile Crescent in southeastern Turkey at around 10,000 BCE. Our outlook is that this archaic influence carried forward in India through the matriarchy of the Sakti (or Shakti) Cult, whose symbology provides a close match for that of Gobekli Tepe. Traditional researchers understand the Sakti Cult to have been a precursor to the Vedic, Buddhist, and Hindu traditions. In our own more speculative studies, we explored likely evidences of that same cult in ancient Egypt at around 4000 BCE in the southern Nile region of Elephantine. We later picked up the apparent trail of many of these same influences in the region of Northern Scotland, where we believe they were exhibited during the later Neolithic era of 3200 BCE. In many different ways, the religious outlook of the Maori bears a close resemblance to the outlooks of people from each of the classic ancient traditions that were instrumental in this progression, and so the Maori creation tradition comes to be of interest to our studies.

Because we believe that the clearest definitions of ancient thought lie with cosmological concepts as they were first understood, priority in these studies has been given to the earliest known forms of words and practices. Likewise, because the cosmologies were commonly framed as an *esoteric tradition* (where inner secrets were revealed to an initiate only after a long period of sustained inquiry), preference is also given to sources known to have devoted many years of study among a given culture. One feature of ancient esoteric traditions such as that of the Dogon is that, in order to protect their innermost secrets, certain facts are known to have been deliberately obfuscated by the priests, especially in the forms in which they were preliminarily told to less-knowledgeable students. Consequently, a trusted initiate who successfully completed the studies might arrive at an understanding of a tradition that could differ markedly from that reported by less-accomplished initiates. To the extent that the broad details of a culture's creation tradition fit the common framework of societies we have already studied, we feel justified in using specific details of those related cosmologies to help point us to the likeliest interpretations.

In the case of the Maori, because the culture itself (and our awareness of it) appears to date from an era that is much more recent than that of, say, ancient Egypt or ancient China, the earliest definitive sources we have for their cosmological concepts are also relatively recent ones. For example, in 1924, after years of life in the bush that had lent themselves to intimate and prolonged study of the Maori culture, Best published *Maori Religion and Mythology,* one of the first (and most extensive) books on the subject of their religion. In the opening page of the book he states, "The subject of the religion of the Maori folk of New Zealand prior to the arrival of Europeans is one of which little is known, owing to the fact that no monograph on the subject has been published."[3]

Since that time, in the nearly one hundred years since the early 1920s, a wealth of research has been undertaken on the Maori culture, in fact so much as to make it, in the words of socio-anthropologist F. Allan Hanson, "one of the most fully documented of those societies traditionally studied by anthropologists."[4] However, Hanson adds that despite this wealth of academic research about the Maori themselves, very little work has been done to try to make their institutions understandable as sensible systems.

Because our approach in this volume is a comparative one, a primary effect of it should be to place the Maori cosmological tradition into a context. Beyond comparisons to outside cultures, whenever possible, we have tried to temper our outlook on any given aspect of the Maori cosmological tradition by comparing the viewpoints of various Maori researchers. In fact, within the body of his early book, Best often provides us with alternate perspectives from various contemporary authorities on Maori life and culture.

One frequently stated outlook of researchers of the Maori is that they had no religion in the modern sense of the word. Best writes, "The ritual pertaining to native gods would not be described as 'prayers' by us, because, in most cases, no supplication appears therein, no benefit or boon is directly asked for, and no act of mercy craved."[5] Best goes on to tell us that the Maori had no regular sacred holidays, that the concept of worship did not seem to pertain to their practices, and that in the Maori culture there was no sense of fear of a deity.

In accordance with the experience of those who have studied with the Dogon, or of ancient Greek philosophers who were reported to have apprenticed themselves to ancient Egyptian priests, Best emphasizes that it is a difficult process to acquire the inner meanings of the Maori tradition, which reside with the more accomplished priests. He remarks that long residence among the tribe, along with a clear understanding of their language, is required for a person to gain the confidence of one of these knowledgeable elders of the tribe.

Over the course of our studies, we have found that important aspects of the ancient cosmology rest in the phonemes that comprise individual words and on the multiple meanings of words that define their concepts. Because of this, as with the other volumes in this series, our expectation is that words of the Maori language will provide us with pivotal clues to the symbolic meanings of ancient cosmological words. In the case of the Maori, we have two primary sources of comparison for these meanings. The first is found in the overt definitions that are given to us by Best during the course of his detailed discussion of the Maori culture, cosmology, and religion. The second comes from a dictionary of the Maori language called *The Maori-Polynesian Comparative Dictionary,* which was compiled by Tregear. He saw very close relationships between the words of the Maori and those of other Polynesian cultures. Given the distances of separation that exist between island groups, it seems likely that somewhat different sets of these meanings may have survived with different cultures. For that reason, we may often assign similar weight to the Polynesian usages of individual words as we do to those of the Maori themselves. Best also offers his own perspectives on the meanings of Maori cosmological terms, which provide a necessary and useful counterpoint to the definitions found in Tregear's Maori dictionary.

To the extent that Maori perspectives on cosmology align with those of other cultures we have studied, comparisons to the languages of those cultures become pertinent. In these cases, we may make reference to Genevieve Calame-Griaule's French dictionary of the Dogon language, called the *Dictionnaire Dogon,* and to Sir E. A. Wallis Budge's *An Egyptian Hieroglyphic Dictionary,* whose word definitions we have long used to correlate to Dogon words and concepts. Although Budge's dictionary has fallen out of favor among many current Egyptologists, its usefulness for our studies is clear. The broad body of well-defined Dogon cosmological words provides us with independent confirmation of Budge's outlook on ancient Egyptian cosmological words.

An understanding of Maori cosmology and language is important to our studies because they seem to preserve links to each important cosmological era and stage that we have explored in prior volumes of this series. Consequently, it would be helpful to understand how those links express themselves before we try to embark on a more in-depth discussion of the Maori system. To the extent that the foundational material may be at times less riveting than the discussion it facilitates, let me express my apologies in advance.

2 Historical Overview of the Esoteric Tradition

Before we begin to evaluate any potential relationship between Maori practices and those of the ancient esoteric tradition we have been pursuing, it makes sense to review the progression of that tradition as we understand it to have unfolded historically. This history is typified by several distinct eras, each with its own likely influences on ancient cultures and each with its own characteristic elements and specific points of reference. Knowledge of these eras and their signature attributes creates a kind of conceptual framework within which to interpret the symbolic elements we encounter in any given culture. The overview we have set down here represents a kind of consensus viewpoint of various cultures whose traditions we have explored, cross-compared, and attempted to reconcile.

Perhaps the greatest threat to the work of a comparative cosmologist lies with his or her own predisposition toward wishful interpretation. The human brain seems essentially "wired" to seek out, find, and try to make sense of patterns, sometimes even in cases where no objective pattern arguably exists. It is on this principle that psychological tools such as the Rorschach test are based. The Rorschach test is the classic psychological exercise in which a person is shown the shape of an inkblot and is asked to interpret the image it presents. The underlying presumption is that the test subject's own internal psychology will cause him or her to perceive the random blob of spilled ink as an image. For a researcher such as myself, the best defense against wishfulness has been to simply impose a rule that, wherever possible, interpretations must begin with an overt statement of how the studied culture perceived a particular concept, symbol, word, or practice. This approach to interpretations offers an even stronger defense against unintended wishfulness when we can demonstrate that two or more cultures with the same practice shared the same understanding of a particular concept or symbol. However, one potential downside to this approach is that it also obliges the researcher to consider any seemingly unlikely interpretations that might be put forth and affirmed by more than one culture.

The earliest cosmological references we can firmly identify in our studies date to the time of the close of the last Ice Age, which places those references in an era sometime prior to 10,000 BCE. Due to the lack of surviving evidence, these kinds of references automatically take on the appearance of being mythical, since they can only have passed down to us through generational stories or through images carved in or painted on stone. Examples of references in this category include Homer's descriptions of the catastrophic sinking of the island continent of Atlantis and claims for the existence of pre–Ice Age cultures such as Mu or Lemuria.

Perhaps the earliest cosmological references that can be objectively evaluated by us originated in the era of Gobekli Tepe, the mountaintop megalithic site in southeastern Turkey, located in the region of the Fertile Crescent. The Gobekli Tepe site is firmly dated by archaeologists to the era of around 10,000 BCE. The site encompasses a diverse set of symbolic elements that include standing stones, megalithic pillars, stone circles with stone benches and stone walls, a wide range of expertly carved animal images, pillars with anthropomorphized features, and several enigmatic symbolic shapes. Among the carved images prominently featured at Gobekli Tepe are animals that later came to be adopted as iconic symbols of deities and monarchs in classic ancient cultures. These include such creatures as birds of prey, scorpions, serpents, and bulls.

During the era of Gobekli Tepe and in the same immediate vicinity, the first evidences of certain civilizing skills make their detectable appearance. These include the cultivation of grains, the domestication of farm animals, the weaving of cloth, the art of pottery, the art of metallurgy and metalworking skills, and stonework and stone carving skills; these are arguably the same set of skills specifically claimed by various ancient cultures as having been imparted to humanity as part of an ancient instructed civilizing plan. Furthermore, the skills appear in proximity to the mountaintop sanctuary of Gobekli Tepe, the same type of setting as is described by ancient cultures for this ancient instruction. The suggestion is that there may have been direct associations between the Gobekli Tepe site, Buddhism's mythical Vulture Peak, where Buddha ostensibly first imparted knowledge to humanity, and the mythical First Time of ancient Egyptian memory, which is referred to as Zep Tepi.

In a previous volume of this series, called *Point of Origin,* we pursued linguistic clues to trace the symbolic elements found at Gobekli Tepe to an archaic matriarchal tradition in India called the Sakti Cult. The cult is understood to have originated in the north and west of India (in the direction of southeastern Turkey and the Fertile Crescent) and to have been ancestral to the Vedic, Buddhist, and Hindu traditions. Language and DNA studies indicate that this cult then spread outward from there in all directions. Evidence of the cult's influence extends as far to the southeast as Australia and as far to the west as Europe. Likely influences of this cult can also be inferred in cultures like predynastic Egypt by around 4000 BCE, most significantly in the region of Elephantine, an island situated at what was originally the first cataract or waterfall of the Nile River.

The Sakti Cult is most closely associated with two Mother Goddesses named Tana Penu and Dharni Penu, twin sisters who together were deemed to be the two mothers of the dancing elephant god Ganesha. Over the centuries, thousands of localized surrogate names were evolved for these goddesses. In later eras, influences of this same cult were evident in relation to the god Siva (or Shiva) and his consort, the goddess Sati, who from the Hindu perspective was also deemed to have been the mother of Ganesha.

It is possible that the Sphinx at Giza could be a remnant of the 10,000 BCE era, since it is thought to have been carved from a natural outcropping of stone and that approach to sculpture was a known practice of the Sakti Cult. The Orion correlation theory of ancient Egypt researcher Robert Bauval proposes that the three largest pyramids at Giza aligned astronomically with the three belt stars of Orion in the era of 10,000 BCE. Some researchers think that the Sphinx was created as a pointer to mark the constellation of Leo in that same era. If we credit those theories, then we are left with only two reasonable possibilities: that at the very least the alignment, if not the actual construction of these structures, did actually date to the era of 10,000 BCE, or else that some later culture was somehow capable of calculating retrospectively what the proper alignments should have been.

By the much later era of 3200 BCE, the construction of a series of megalithic structures was initiated on Orkney Island in Northern Scotland, the earliest ones linked by a road to the Neolithic farming village of Skara Brae. In a previous volume of this series, *The Mystery of Skara Brae,* we argued that these structures were of a cosmological nature and were intended to reflect (on a life-size scale) the same progressive stages of creation that are reflected in the base plan of a Buddhist *stupa* shrine. The suggestion is that these Orkney Island structures constituted a kind of walk-through training ground for concepts of cosmology and that the island itself might have been compared to a kind of college campus. Associated with these megalithic sites was a set of eight stone houses at Skara Brae, set alongside an actual working farm, that we believe served as housing for class-groups of initiates and their families. Our outlook is that, during the period from 3200 BCE to 2600 BCE, this farm was used to instruct these same initiates in the skills of agriculture. Orkney Island is situated at the northernmost flow of the mid-Atlantic Ocean currents and hosts easily navigated harbors.

The implication is that groups from various regions of the world may have been brought to this very accessible, campus-like setting in order to be trained in civilizing skills.

Shortly thereafter, at around 3100 BCE, monarchies, founded on functional systems of agriculture, began to appear in various regions of the globe. These included the emergence of dynastic kingship in Egypt, the appearance of the earliest emperors in China, and likely kingships in Ireland and Peru. At about that same time, distinct revisions or reversals occurred in the form of ancient cosmological symbols and concepts. Archaic matriarchal religious traditions came to be supplanted by patriarchal traditions. Creator gods such as Ra and Amen in Egypt and Siva in India came to take precedence over long-revered Mother Goddesses. These changes crossed cultural boundaries and so seem to reflect the action of some regionally capable (or perhaps even globally capable) influence.

At around this same time, symbolic systems of writing first came into use, often flatly claimed by the cultures who adopted them as having been gifts from the gods. Many of the early glyph images took the form of well-defined cosmological shapes from a preexisting orally transmitted esoteric tradition and were often understood to represent the same cosmological meanings. Fundamental similarities can be shown to have existed between the first symbolic written languages in ancient Egypt and in ancient China, where certain hieroglyphic words were formulated in matching ways. Cosmological information that had long been passed from generation to generation as part of an oral tradition began to be placed in writing and was now passed down generationally in the form of written texts.

At about 1500 BCE, the first evidence of monotheistic religion (in the modern sense) appeared. The massive eruption of Thera on the island of Santorini in the Aegean Sea near Greece, which occurred around this time, is seen by some to relate historically to the biblical story of Moses and the Exodus from Egypt. It is also the approximate era of the Egyptian pharaoh Akhnaten and his efforts to establish monotheistic religion during the Eighteenth Dynasty in ancient Egypt.

According to Dogon and Buddhist sources, the ancient civiliz-ing plan was intimately linked to a creation tradition, and each of the instructed civilizing skills was tagged to a concept or process of cre-ation. The associated symbolic concepts pertained to three distinct creational themes: the formation of the universe, the formation of mat-ter, and the processes of biological reproduction. These three themes represented processes that were conceptually parallel and were seen as being so fundamentally similar to one another that, within the ancient tradition, they could be described using a single progression of symbols. Consequently, any given symbol might carry specific nuances of mean-ing in relation to each of the three creational themes. For example, just as the processes of biological reproduction begin with a *fertilized egg,* so the formation of the universe was conceived of as beginning with a *cosmogonic egg.* Likewise, the processes that initiate the formation of matter were said to begin with a figure akin to the Egyptian and Chinese *sun glyph,* ☉, which the Dogon characterize as the *egg-in-a-ball.*

In the ancient cosmology, creation is said to rest on two fundamen-tal principles, those of *duality* and *the pairing of opposites.* The processes of biological creation clearly illustrate these two principles: during bio-logical reproduction, a fertilized egg results when a *feminine energy* (in the form of a woman's unfertilized egg) comes together with a *mascu-line energy* (in the form of a man's sperm.) From this perspective, the processes of biological life are catalyzed by an act of *conception* that pro-motes the union of these two elements—an event that, in the mind-set of the cosmology, is characterized as an *embrace.* By comparison, the processes of the formation of matter are said to rest on a similar set of principles: our material universe is seen as a *masculine energy* and is said to be paired with a nonmaterial universe that is conceptualized as a *feminine energy.* An act of *perception* unites the two energies in an *embrace,* comparable to that of biological conception, which is then understood to catalyze the processes of the formation of matter.

During the archaic period from 10,000 BCE until the first

appearance of written language around 3000 BCE, the symbolic meanings of the cosmology were passed down orally and resided with a base set of root phonetic values, rather than written glyphs. Relationships between cosmological words appear to have been defined based on common pronunciation, rather than (as modern Egyptologists often infer) on similarity of glyph structure. Permutations of these root phonemes are evident in the languages of the various groups we have studied, and the possible shades of meaning they convey become more evident as we explore and compare the words of additional cultures who shared aspects of the same cosmology. The consistency with which the phonemes can be shown to relate to the intended meaning often makes it possible to predict the cosmological implications of a given word based solely on its phonetic structure.

Included among these symbolic phonemes were:

ak = light
am = knowledge (or the biblical notion of conception)
ar = ascension
ba = place, soul, or spirit
da = mother
de or *di* = to apprehend or learn
ga = doorway or gate, or empty of
ia = existence
ji = vibration
ka = duality or the concept of an embrace
ke = nonexistence coming into existence
ma = sight or perception
mu = ancestor
na = woman or feminine relative
nu = water or waves
pa = ancestor
pe = mouth or the concept of space
po = atom or matter

ra = symbolic of the sun, gravity, and the material universe

sa = Orion

si = symbolic of Sirius and the nonmaterial universe

ta = earth or mass

va = speak or say

ve or *vi* = to come

yi = transformation or a change in the physical state of something

These and other significant phonemes were then combined with one another to define larger words and to express more complex concepts. For example, someone with an awareness of how these phonemes work might have recognized that the Dogon term *nummo* was likely to combine the root phonemes *nu* and *ma* and so implied the notion of matter in its wavelike state being perceived. The first name of the Sakti Earth Mother goddess Tana Penu combines the phonemes *ta* ("earth") and *na* ("mother"). The Chinese term *yijing* or *i ching* (which we interpret as referring to the changes that matter in its wavelike state goes through as it is transformed into particles) combines the phonemes *yi* ("change in the state of something") and *ji* ("vibration"). Knowledge of how these phonemes worked in various ancient cultures to create cosmological words can give us a significant head start when trying to interpret the cosmological words of an as-yet unfamiliar culture.

It is of great benefit to our studies that the Dogon place a very high priority on the purity of language and take great care with their definition and pronunciation. In the opinion of Edward Shortland, a nineteenth-century doctor and linguist who studied the Maori, the same can be said to be true of them. He writes in *Maori Religion and Mythology,* "The *Maori* language is essentially conservative, containing no principle in its structure facilitating change. The component parts or roots of words are always apparent."[1]

One pivotal aspect of the archaic cosmology as it has survived in various cultures rests on a set of *complex phonemes* that could carry two or more different pronunciations when used under different circumstances. Over time, these seemed to have retained one phonetic form for some cultures and another form for others. At least four of these complex phonemes are still recognized within the Hebrew language, and the Kabbalists actually recognize the existence of seven dual letters in Hebrew.[2] The net consequence of these phonemes being used for various words of our cosmology is that to properly correlate words between two cultures, we may need to look on these phonetic values as being functionally equivalent to one another. For example, ancient root words for "elephant" may be pronounced *pil* or *fil*. An archaic word for "temple" may be pronounced *get*, *het*, or even *chet* or *chait*. Furthermore, certain phonetic sounds seem not to have been represented in certain languages, and so a predictable set of alternate phonemes may sometimes be substituted. For example, an *R* in the language of one culture might be expressed as an *L* or as a *W* by another. What this means for our studies is that we must allow a certain amount of "wiggle room" as we explore likely resemblances between the cosmological words of various cultures.

3 Deities of the Maori Pantheon

In *Maori Religion and Mythology,* Best includes an introductory chapter about the Maori pantheon of gods and goddesses, titled "The Gods of the Maori." As may be familiar to us from the cosmologies of other cultures like ancient Greece, this pantheon is conceptualized within the framework of a family lineage. Specific details of how each of these deities related to one another ancestrally can vary from source to source, based on the sometimes contradictory information relayed by different myths, texts, or priests. From Best's perspective, these deities fit within a hierarchical structure and so can be conceptualized into distinct classes, almost akin to the zoological families and orders of animals. As we discuss the specific deified personalities, we should keep in mind Best's view that the Maori did not actually worship these deities in the modern sense of the word. Rather, the characters should be seen to represent concepts, stages, and aspects of the processes of creation that have come to be personified so as to metaphorically illustrate these processes within mythic storylines.

Io

If we accept Best's views on these deities, the Maori pantheon begins with a god named Io, who constituted the Supreme Being and so stood in a class by himself. Best tells us that the cult of Io was known only to the higher classes of Maori priests, and so knowledge of him constituted esoteric knowledge that a beginning initiate would only eventually come to attain. From a scientific perspective, the innermost aspects of cosmology touch on concepts that, placed in the wrong hands, could prove destructive. Consequently, the intentions of the initiate became a key factor in admission to the cult. Best tells us that "the practice of this cult and that of . . . black magic, by the same person was not permissible in some districts."[1] Knowledge that fell into this restricted category was referred to by the word *tapu,* a term that is a likely correlate to the more generally familiar word *taboo.* Tregear defines the word *tapu* to mean "under restriction" or "prohibited."[2]

Tregear defines *Io* as "God, the Supreme Being."[3] The consensus Maori view is that Io was responsible for begetting the major deities of the Maori pantheon. As was true for deities in the ancient traditions of Egypt, China, India, and elsewhere, a list of honorific titles was assigned to Io, each of which emphasized aspects of the cosmological roles he played. Once again, depending on the source of the list, the specific titles given, the order in which they were presented, and the Maori terms used to characterize them all could vary.

Best considers the Maori tradition of Io to be an exceedingly ancient one and dismisses suggestions that similarities to later religions could be the result of more modern Christian influences on the Maori. In support of that view, he cites the archaic forms of language used in the various Maori texts from which the information was drawn and points to the lack of preservation in the Maori texts of recognizable phraseology from the Old Testament, beyond that of the Book of Genesis.

Best also unhesitatingly compares various attributes assigned to Io to those of deities from other ancient traditions. For example, he relates the Maori notion that Io was "the beginning of the gods" to "the old Egyptian concept of the Supreme Being."[4] Likewise, one set of titles of Io, given as "Io of the hidden face" or "Io at the hidden place," could seem to associate Io with the hidden gods Amma and Amen of the Dogon and of ancient Egypt. Best states that in the Maori view, Io could not be seen, and he cites the "hidden" titles as evidence to support that view. He suggests that only Io's radiance or glow could reportedly be seen by humans. To underscore the idea, Best quotes a Hellenistic Jewish philosopher named Philo, who wrote, "God is invisible, for how can eyes that are too weak to gaze upon the sun be strong enough to gaze upon its maker."[5]

Significantly, Best mentions sources who compare the Maori concept of Io to the ancient god "Iahoue or Iahveh." One source states that, in other ancient cultures, these names "became contracted into Iahou or Io."[6] In defense of that view, Best writes, "The Maori concept of Io bears a strong resemblance to that of Jahweh among the Semites with regard to the lack of any definite ideas of the Supreme Being. No images of that being were made, and the great is surrounded by mystery, vagueness, and intense *tapu*."[7]

In summary, the Maori concept of Io was that of a Supreme Being, a creator who was himself uncreated, had no parents, was never born and never dies, and had no offspring (notwithstanding Maori myths that credit him with having begotten other gods). Best categorically dismisses suggestions that Io might have been a human ancestor who later came to be deified. Despite all of this, the Maori made no offerings to Io and lacked most of the aspects of worship toward Io that we would associate with the deity of a modern religion.

Rangi and Papa

Because of differences that exist in the genealogical tables of deities given by various Maori sources, a definitive mythic lineage from Io, the Supreme Being, to the Sky Parents Rangi and Papa cannot be precisely stated. In other creation traditions we have studied, the processes of creation, once initiated, reach a point of culmination with the separation of *earth* and *sky,* concepts that were often anthropomorphized in the form of *primal parents*. For the Maori, Rangi (who is termed "the greatest father of all men") represented the concept of *the heavens* or *sky,* while his female counterpart or consort Papa was considered the Great Mother and symbolized the *earth.* This symbolism is the reverse of what we encounter in the earliest cosmological traditions of cultures like ancient China. A certain amount of gender confusion relating to these symbolic assignments is apparent in the traditional meanings of related Maori words. For example, as in the familiar modern usage, *papa* was an affectionate Maori term for "father" and so suggests a preexisting symbolic aspect for the term that would be masculine, not feminine. Likewise, a character from Maori mythology named Rangiuru, whose name is formulated on a masculine term, was described as a mother and a wife.

Tane

Best refers to the second class of Maori deities as *departmental gods.* He defines these as gods who take anthropomorphic form and who are deemed to have presided over certain arts, industries, and natural productions. Because of the way that the esoteric tradition of the Maori concealed its inner secrets, these deified constructs represented the highest echelon of gods known to the ordinary Maori people. In Best's estimation, Tane was "assuredly the most important being" of the class of departmental gods.[8] Best feels that this fact was clearly demonstrated by the importance of the activities Tane performed within the mythos of the tradition. Best describes him as "the most conspicuous of the offspring of the primal parents." In Maori mythology, it is Tane who ascended to the domain of the Supreme Being Io in order to acquire three baskets or receptacles of esoteric knowledge, which were considered to be of the greatest value to humanity. Tane is the god who reportedly succeeded in turning back the powers of darkness. From this perspective, Best considers Tane to represent the concept of *light.* Tane was also intimately associated with the concept of agriculture in that he was considered the *author of all vegetation.*[9]

Tane was understood to have been the originator of birds, a class of creatures that play important symbolic roles in the cosmology and history of many ancient cultures. These notably include birds of prey, such as the hawk, which hold symbolic significance from the era of Gobekli Tepe onward. From a linguistic perspective, all of the mythical offspring of Tane are associated with bird names. Moreover, he was credited with having created the first woman and so played a key ancestral role in relation to humanity.

From yet another perspective of Maori mythology, Tane held importance as a member of the Polynesian trinity of Tane, Tu, and Rongo. This outlook potentially aligns him cosmologically with the symbolism of a triad of astronomic bodies (the Sirius stars, the belt stars of Orion, and Barnard's Loop) that are significant in the creation traditions of other cultures we have studied. As part of this widely known trinity, it makes sense that each of the deities that comprise it would be comparably well known throughout Polynesia.

Tu

Among the most knowledgeable of the Maori priests, Tu plays the role of a *destroyer,* comparable to the symbolism of the god Shiva in the Hindu tradition. This mythical role reinforces our presumption of an association between Tu and Barnard's Loop, the spiraling astronomic structure that, for the Dogon, serves as a kind of macrocosmic counterpart to the microcosmic egg-of-the-world and whose rotation may evoke notions of cyclical destruction. The name *Tu* forms the phonetic root of a Maori term *tumau,* which means "fixed" or "constant."[10] This word would seem to be a clear correlate to an important cosmological term of the Dogon (*toymu*) and the ancient Egyptian (*temau*) that relates to the formation of the egg-of-the-world and implies the notion of *completeness.* Taken in the context of the Hebrew word *shiva,* which means "seven," symbolic correlations to the god Shiva uphold the numerology of the seven-chambered structure (discussed in more detail in *Sacred Symbols of the Dogon,* beginning on page 35). Likewise, Tu carries symbolism in Polynesian mythology that links him to concepts of death, war, and the underworld. Likewise, there are perspectives from which Tu can relate to the idea of the *setting sun,* a notion that in ancient Egyptian culture was also closely associated with death and the Underworld, which was also known as the Tuat. Similar setting-sun symbolism was assigned to the Egyptian god Tem or Tum, whose name also conjures the concept of temau. Although Tu is consistently cast as a male god in most regions of Polynesia, Best tells us that some groups considered Tu to be a goddess. This gender confusion again seems reflective of reversals in symbolism that seem to have emerged cross-regionally within the cosmology sometime after 3200 BCE.

Rongo

Rongo is the third member of the trinity of Maori deities that is associated with Tane and Tu. Tregear suggests that, although Rongo was paid reverence universally throughout Polynesia, his attributes differ widely in different Polynesian locales. According to Best, Rongo's symbolic aspects in Maori mythology relate to agriculture and to peacefulness, and emphasize hospitality, generosity, and courtesy. As such, concepts personified by Rongo certainly reflect aspects of ancient civilizing instruction as they are understood by the Dogon and other cultures. However, Best tells us that agricultural operations were classed among the secretive processes of the Maori culture, and so he also associates Rongo with the esoteric instruction that initiates to the Maori tradition received.[11] Rongo was considered the protector of crops in the Maori culture, and appeals were made to him to guarantee that an agricultural crop would be abundant. Best sees evidence that Rongo was originally a *lord of abundance* who was honored alongside Tane. However, the earliest references illustrate that he personified a process that would have preceded the harvesting of grown crops. Perhaps the best Egyptian conceptual correlate to Rongo would be a goddess of the harvest named Rennutt, whose name rests on the phonetic root *rennu*, which means "to harvest" and implies "joy, rejoicing, and gladness."[12]

Tangaroa

Tangaroa is described by Best as "an important departmental being."[13] Although he is traditionally seen as a personified incarnation of the ocean, there are suggestions that his symbolism may relate to an important Dogon cosmological drawing called the *nummo fish*. Support for that view is upheld by a Maori outlook that views Tangaroa as the "personified form of fish."[14] The Dogon image is a kind of stick-figure outline that bears a resemblance to a catfish. Based on definitions given by the Dogon priests, the component attributes of the fish, which include a central heart, two collarbones, two fins, a squared head, and four whiskers, seem to symbolically depict the events that pertain to the perception of matter in its wavelike state, which initiate the formation of matter.

As we understand the Dogon drawing conceptually, an act of perception (centered at the heart of the nummo fish) causes the "perfect

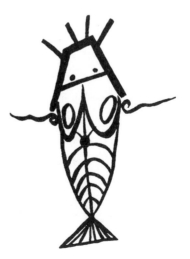

Dogon nummo fish drawing
(from Griaule and Dieterlen,
The Pale Fox, 185)

order" of the waves (the scales of the lower body) to be disrupted and drawn upward (a concept conveyed by the collarbones, or clavicles, of the fish), then afterward to be extended and effectively reassembled into what we see as particles of matter. (The head of the nummo fish takes the pyramidal shape of a squared hemisphere, symbolizing the concept of *mass*.) In accordance with that scenario, the Maori word *tanga* means "to be assembled or congregated,"[15] while the Maori word *roa* means "length" or "extension."[16] On one level of interpretation, the differentiation of matter into particles is what is referred to by the idea of *multiplicity* emerging from *unity*. Consistent with these outlooks, in Maori cosmology fish are understood to have originated with the son of Tangaroa, whose two-word name implies the concepts of *numbers* and *multitude*.[17] A Maori saying that pertains to Tangaroa, given as *He wai Tangaroa i haere ai ki uta*, translates as, "By means of water, Tangaroa was enabled to go inland."

Best cites the existence of a "singular myth" of the Maori concerning Tangaroa, a god more formally named Rua-te-pupuke, whose name means "two" or "repetition," which implies *immediacy*. He is understood to be one of a broader class of gods called Rua, who are taken to be "the personified forms of knowledge and its acquisition"[18] and so are effective correlates to the concept of *an act of perception*. Variant versions of the myth are repeated, but the upshot is that, like particles from waves of mass, Tangaroa is drawn upward out of the ocean and placed on the roof of a house. An event of destruction or tragedy follows, after which Rua banishes Tangaroa to the ocean. Best makes the comment that "this peculiar myth probably contains some hidden meaning unknown to us."[19] In some Polynesian localities such as Tahiti, Tangaroa was celebrated as the original creator god who formed the islands of the Pacific and caused them to rise from the deep. In other situations, there were associations between Tangaroa and the moon, which might possibly arise from the moon's role in inducing ocean tides.

Tawhiri-Matea

Best defines Tawhiri-Matea as the deity who was in charge of the *winds*. In the language of our cosmology, *wind* is a symbolic term for the concept of *vibration*. From a scientific perspective, any given vibration is defined by the frequency of its wavelength. Appropriate to those definitions, Tregear defines the Maori word *tawhiri* as meaning "to wave to" or "to beckon." In addition to this personification of wind as a generic concept, each wind (north, south, east, and west) also had its personified form. Best notes that there were also many names presented in Maori mythology for what are referred to as *wind children*.[20] In the framework of the cosmological analogy, these might well relate to the multiple vibrational frequencies of particles of matter.

Maori myths relate that when the offspring of Rangi and Papa made the decision to separate their parents, earth and sky, Tawhiri-Matea was the only one who objected to the choice. Scientifically speaking, the growth of particles of matter is accompanied by the force of *gravity,* whose pull would have tended to resist the separation of massed bodies as the concept of space initially emerged. Appropriate to that outlook, the Maori myth then tells us that Rongo, Tangaroa, and Tu attempted to force the Sky Parent upward but failed in that attempt. Ultimately, it was Tane who succeeded in accomplishing the separation. Tane, who on one level symbolizes the male energy associated with *mass,* also bears a relationship to the scientific concept of an *orbit,* the cosmological effect that sustains a separation of distance between two astronomic bodies. During these events, Tangaroa is said to have taken refuge in the waters of the ocean, and a few of his lizard-like children, known as the *repulsive ones,* took refuge on land. The use of the term *repulsive* in the context of this myth serves to confirm an interpretation that could relate to the force of gravity.

Haumia

Some versions of the tribal myths of the Maori include a character named Haumia as one of the offspring of the primal parents, Rangi and Papa. Best is of the opinion that Haumia represents the *aruhe*, edible roots of a fern plant that was important to the food supply of the Maori. The significant mythical act that Haumia is credited with is having taken root in the Earth following the separation of the Earth and Sky Parents. In Dogon cosmology, one of the conceptual metaphors that is given for the creation of matter is framed in relation to the growth of a plant from a seed. It is possible that this poorly understood aspect of Maori cosmology related to a similar metaphor. In the ancient Chinese cosmological tradition, the term *hao* referred to a structure comparable to the Dogon egg-of-the-world. We see this as a correlate to the *Calabi-Yau space* of *string theory*. From this perspective, the structure would specifically be an end product of processes that differentiate mass (earth) and space (sky).

Whiro

It is Best's belief that the Maori departmental god Whiro represented the concepts of *darkness* and *evil*. Some researchers of Maori mythology compare Whiro's symbolic association with an evil spirit to scriptural accounts of Lucifer.[21]

From other mythological perspectives, Whiro was considered to be the older brother of Tane, since the cosmological condition of *darkness* is traditionally understood to have preceded the condition of *light*. Tregear's dictionary entry for the god's name informs us that, in Maori myth, Whiro was banished as a consequence of an improper intimacy he formed with the wife of one of his nephews.

From a cosmological perspective, *duality* is seen as a principle of creation, and yet the processes of the creation of matter are each described as having been initiated by a single act, such as an act of perception or the rupturing of a cosmogonic egg. One way of representing this type of exception to the rule of duality is by comparing it to a sexual act that involves only one person or that is in some way considered to be improper. For example, in the Dogon and Egyptian traditions, the processes of creation can be described as having begun with a masturbatory or incestuous act.

By comparison, Dogon cosmology also includes an episode of impropriety, but it is expressed in relation to a storyline in which one of the eight mythical Dogon ancestors was said to have descended to Earth out of his proper sequence. According to the Dogon myth, the first six ancestors made their appearances according to their numerology, but for reasons that are not fully explained, the eighth came down before the seventh. This breach of protocol so angered the seventh ancestor that he killed the eighth ancestor. (The French anthropologist Marcel Griaule, who exhaustively documented the Dogon creation tradition, questioned his Dogon informant, the priest Ogotemmeli, on this point, and it was admitted that the reference is meant to be symbolic, not historic, and so no Dogon ancestor was actually killed.) A deeper exploration of the Dogon symbolism shows that it relates to what the Dogon consider to be an inherent flaw in our material universe, one that pertains to the structure of the spiraling egg-of-the-world on which all larger structures of matter are based. An alternate meaning for the Maori word *whiro* suggests that this episode of Maori mythology might well relate to a similar cosmological concept, since in common usage, *whiro* can mean "to spin," "to twist," or "to plait."

Ru (or Ruaumoko)

The youngest of seventy Maori offspring of Rongo and Papa was Ru (sometimes called Ruaumoko). Tregear lists the full name of Ru as Ru-wai-moko-roa. The Maori word *ru* means "to shake,"[22] *wai* means "water,"[23] the word *moko* refers to "tattoo marks on the face or body,"[24] and the word *roa* implies the concept of "length" or "extension."[25] The cosmological implication is that of matter in its wavelike state having been extended to create a kind of hidden face. Comparable symbolism is associated with the Dogon practice of creating carved wooden masks. Ruaumoko is understood to have been so young at the time when the pivotal events of creation occurred that he was still a suckling infant of the Earth Mother and so never emerged into the upper world that constitutes our material reality.[26] So it is understandable that his symbolism relates to the subterranean world and concepts of darkness, and that he was understood to act as a protector of the spirits of the dead, whose traditional cosmological domain is the underworld.

4 Parallels to Dogon Cosmology

Our initial entry point to the study of ancient cosmology was a modern-day primitive African tribe from Mali called the Dogon. They are a priestly tribe from a remote desert region of Northwest Africa, situated in southern Mali. The Dogon have long lived in relative isolation from the outside world, and it is clear that the choice to do so was a deliberate one. Living at a distance from outside influences is consistent with a Dogon cultural mind-set that prioritizes the preservation of ancient rituals, civic practices, cultural outlook, and language. Outwardly, the Dogon are farmers, weavers, artists, mask makers, and priests; however, they also preserve a complex symbolic creation tradition. The initial impulse to focus our inquiries about ancient cosmology on the Dogon turns out to have been a fortuitous one, since their culture integrates important elements from a number of different classic ancient traditions.

We have seen that Dogon civic practices bear a consistent resemblance to those known to have existed in ancient Egypt. Like the Egyptians, the Dogon establish their villages and districts in pairs called *upper* and *lower*. A Dogon chieftain is referred to by the term *faro*, comparable to the Egyptian title of pharaoh. The Dogon use the same set of diverse calendars as the ancient Egyptians, including solar and lunar calendars, a 360-day civic calendar, an agricultural calendar, and a calendar related to the planet Venus. However, Dogon society consistently

31

reflects Egyptian practices as they were known to have existed in a very early period of Egyptian culture, seemingly from around the boundary between predynastic and dynastic times in Egypt. Consequently, Dogon society is lacking certain familiar elements of Egyptian culture that are understood to have developed sometime after 2900 BCE. These include the use of five intercalary (leap-year) days to reconcile time frames in their calendars and evidence of a written language.

Although the Dogon have no indigenous written language, the words that define their creation tradition are demonstrably ancient Egyptian words. Much attention has been devoted in prior volumes of this series to correlating Dogon words and meanings to Egyptian hieroglyphic words and meanings. In keeping with Dogon rituals that reflect Jewish practices, many of these same words also have likely correlates in the Hebrew language. The system of concepts and symbols that comprise Dogon cosmology, however, most closely matches the tradition that is associated with an aligned ritual Buddhist shrine called a stupa. In fact, the Dogon system is also defined in relation to an aligned ritual shrine whose form is very much like that of a Buddhist stupa. The close similarities of these two systems allow us to cross-confirm the meanings of cosmological concepts and relationships to specific symbols. Because the Buddhist cosmology is given in Sanskrit words that can take distinctly different forms than Egyptian or Dogon words, it seems unlikely that either the Dogon or the Buddhists simply adopted their tradition wholesale from the other.

As we have suggested, Dogon ritual practices also bear a close resemblance to Judaism in that the Dogon wear skullcaps and prayer shawls, circumcise their young, and celebrate a Jubilee Year. Their tribal culture is organized according to revered family lineages, comparable to what we find in Judaism. For example, the Hogon priests of the Dogon tribe compare to the priestly Cohane clan of Judaism, and the descendants of a mythical Dogon ancestor named Lebe compare to the Levi tribe of Judaism. Conceptually, as we approach the inner definitions of the Dogon cosmological tradition, abiding parallels can be seen to the Kabbalistic tradition of Judaism.

Linguists say that the Dogon language is not easily classifiable because it includes a number of distinct subgroups of words that were drawn from different languages. Thus far in our cosmological studies, we have offered correlations to Dogon words from various languages, including the Egyptian hieroglyphic language, Hebrew, the Dravidian languages of the Tamil (a cultural group that is thought to have originated to the northwest of India), the Turkish language, the Dongba language of the Na-Khi tribe in Tibet, and even ancient Chinese. From the standpoint of cosmology, we have demonstrated broad agreement between Dogon words and Egyptian hieroglyphic words, and so the two languages provide us with valuable cross-confirmation of the likely pronunciations and meanings of many cosmological words.

Notwithstanding the great geographic distance between North Africa and New Zealand, Dogon references become pertinent to our study of Maori cosmology once we realize that many of the characteristic attributes of the Maori religion are also reflected in the religion of the Dogon. As in the Dogon culture, Best tells us that Maori myth and religion are closely intertwined and that precepts of the religion essentially defined the contours of everyday life among the Maori.[1] He describes the Maori religion as being both *cosmogonic* (pertaining to the origin of the universe) and *anthropogenic* (pertaining to the development of the human race). Once again, this is just as we observe the situation to be in the Dogon tradition.[2] Best characterizes the esoteric tradition of the Maori in terms that relate directly to what we know about the Dogon tradition, saying that the education of an initiate to the Maori esoteric tradition could be a lengthy process and that to attain an innermost level of knowledge required the initiate to gain the intimate confidence of a tribal elder.[3]

Tregear writes in his 1904 book *The Maori Race,* "When attempting to question an old priest on the subject of the ancient Maori worship of the Supreme Being he was refused information, and politely referred to another priest 100 miles away. Probably that priest would have referred him again to someone else and so on. Each initiate into the sacred mysteries considered his knowledge as a trust to be guarded against the outer world, and it is only under most exceptional circumstances that information could be acquired."[4]

Consistent with the archaic philosophies that underlie the Dogon religion, the Maori religion was not rooted in traditional Christian concepts of heaven and hell or of an afterlife, although the concepts of both a soul and a spiritual or nonmaterial realm were defined. Again, Tregear writes in *The Maori Race,* "The great difference between the conception of the Maori Spirit World and our own is that the native idea had nothing therein of the future life being a state where reward or punishment was meted out according to the quality of the mortal life."[5]

We know that the Dogon often illustrate concepts of creation through the defined actions of characters in myths. However, unlike Egyptian culture (but consistent with earlier traditions), they do not personify these concepts as anthropomorphized deities. Best writes, "The Maori have viewed the powers of nature as concrete in one meaning of that term, as opposed to abstract, but there is nothing to show that he viewed them as entities. He personified them in obedience to his mythopoetic nature, as he personified the ocean, earth, sky, as also misfortune, sickness, death, etc."[6]

Best goes on to say that natural phenomena can be treated as entities in Maori cosmology in the sense that the evolution of stages of creation from "empty space down to the appearance of earth and sky" is presented in the form of a genealogy. This perspective aligns well with how the Dogon treat their symbolic concept of *ancestors.* Another commentator on the Maori, a German professor and parson by the name of Ferdinand von Hochstetter, echoed Best's characterization of the Maori tradition as one without traditional worshipped deities. He described the Maori religion as "a kind of polytheism" or "worship of elementary spirits and deified ancestors; yet without idols and temples."[7] Once again, the notion of ancestors is one that plays an essential role in Dogon cosmology, both in a literal and a symbolic sense. Best adds the statement, "Some consider that all Maori gods were deified ancestors."[8]

We are also told that the Maori, again like the Dogon, defined two distinct classes of myths. The first were somewhat akin to stories that are told around a campfire. These can be thought of as constituting public myths, which were known to any member of the tribe. In the Dogon culture, myths of this kind work to establish the basic storylines and symbolic elements of the cosmology, concepts that ultimately frame a more secret body of knowledge, open only to trusted initiates. They also serve to orient the average tribe member to the mind-set of the cosmological tradition and to foster interest in learning about it.

Like the Dogon, the Maori understand that creation emerged in stages, and they define a series of discrete steps for the process. Like many of the other cultures we study, the Maori associate these stages with the ordinal numbers (even in Christianity, God is One), and so any recitation of the stages of creation in their proper sequence could be compared to the act of counting. In *China's Cosmological Prehistory,* we commented on similar associations between the stages of creation and the ordinal numbers in the early creation traditions of ancient China. These become evident both in the yijing and in Daoism. We see the survival of similar symbolism in Judaism, where creation is said to have happened over the course of seven days and where the first six days are simply assigned numbers, given as Day 1, Day 2, and so on. The sequence ends with the Sabbath, a term that we associate with the number seven.

Maori names for the stages of creation center on the term *Kore,* or *Te Kore,* a word that, according to Tregear, refers to "the primal power of the Cosmos, the Void or negation, yet containing the potentiality of all things afterwards to come."[9] Best says that the generic term *te kore* signifies "non-existence," "non-possession," or "non-occurrence."[10] In the view of the ancient cosmology, prior to these creative processes all reality exists as a perfectly ordered *unity.* The stages of creation are seen as the process by which *multiplicity* emerges from *unity* through successive divisions. So it makes sense that an alternate definition of the word *Kore* is given to mean "broken; a break, a fracture."[11]

Dogon words formed from the root *ko* provide us with some potential insights into possible meanings of the Maori term *Kore.* The Dogon word *koro* refers to a source of water and means "to surround."[12] From a cosmological perspective, these meanings describe matter in its base state as primordial waves that are drawn up by an act of perception and then twist and loop in such a way as to surround and define empty space. These looping dimensions are said to create a primary unit of matter that the Dogon call the egg-in-a-ball, or the *po pilu.* Other Dogon definitions describe the term *koro* as referring to an "empty container" or a "bucket to transport earth." Within the framework of the cosmology, the term *earth* is symbolic of the concept of mass or matter.

Einstein's theory of relativity, based on his famous formula $E = mc^2$, implies that the *speed of light* remains a constant as mass or acceleration increases. The only way this could be possible would be if the *time frame* slows down as acceleration or mass increases. In other words, time would pass more slowly for someone who was moving at speeds very close to the speed of light than it would for us in our everyday lives. This perspective implies that matter in its primordial wavelike state, in which it is virtually massless, must exist within the context of an ultrafast time frame by comparison to ours. Essentially, within the void of *primordial waves* where mass effectively does not exist, all events must effectively occur at once. In keeping with that outlook, the Dogon phoneme *ko* means "immediate" and so suggests that, on one level, the cosmic void of Te Kore might refer to a "place of immediacy." Supportive of this interpretation is the Maori view that any recitation of the stages of creation can also be looked on as an enumeration of the "aeons of time."[13]

In Dogon cosmology, instructed civilizing concepts are symbolically defined as *words,* and the words are presented in relation to a sequence of ordinal numbers. So when Griaule wrote about the steps of his instruction as a Dogon initiate, he organized the chapters of his book *Dieu d'Eau* (God of Water, or in the English-language edition, *Conversations with Ogotemmeli*) in relation to numbered *words*. Griaule explained that in the Dogon tradition, instructed civilizing skills were tagged in parallel to successive stages of creation. The *First Word* related to the concept of clothing, the *Second Word* to concepts of weaving, and so on. So it may be significant that the Maori word *Kore* bears both a conceptual and a phonetic relationship to the Egyptian word *kher,* meaning "word."[14] As in the ancient Hebrew language, when Egyptian hieroglyphic words were written, vowel sounds were omitted. Consequently, the precise pronunciation of any Egyptian hieroglyphic word can only be approximated. A vowel-less Egyptian word given essentially as *k-h-r* might have been pronounced *kher,* as Budge interpreted it, or might conceivably have been pronounced *khore.*

Meanwhile, the Dogon egg-of-the-world, the structure that is the product of the progressive stages of matter, is also characterized as the *Word.* The implication is that this is the fundamental unit on which a metaphorically "spoken" creation is formed. The Maori word *te* means "the."[15] From that perspective, the compound term *Te Kore* would imply a meaning of "the Word." From Best's perspective, the generic term *te kore* signifies the concept of "nonexistence."[16]

Best provides a list of the stages of Te Kore on page 34 of his *Maori Religion and Mythology,* which we re-create below. The name of each stage is prefixed by "Te Kore," perhaps implying "the Word."

> Te Kore tuatahi—the first Kore
> Te Kore tuarua—the second Kore
> Te Kore tuatoru—the third Kore
> Te Kore tuawha—the fourth Kore
> Te Kore tuarima—the fifth Kore
> Te Kore tuaono—the sixth Kore
> Te Kore tuawhitu—the seventh Kore
> Te Kore tuawaru—the eighth Kore
> Te Kore tuaiwa—the ninth Kore
> Te Kore tuangahuru—the tenth Kore

According to Best, the first stage of Te Kore was called *tuatahi*. The Maori word *tuatahi* means "first."[17] In keeping with the symbolism that relates to numbers and counting previously discussed, Tregear explains that *tua* is an ordinal prefix that can be attached to adjectives to express numeric concepts of sequence like "first" or "second."[18] (If we attach the prefix *tua* to the Maori word for "one," which is *tahi,* the combined term is *tuatahi,* which means "first.") Tregear also tells us that the Maori word *tua* is a religious word that implies "indefinite power and infinity."[19] The word *tua* also represents the root phoneme from which the Maori word *atua,* meaning "god," is formed. Tregear associates the words *tua* and *atua* with the Hawaiian phoneme *kua* and word *akua,* meaning "god." From our previous studies, we know that the Egyptian term *ak* or *aakhu* (Dogon *ogo*) refers to the concept of *light* and that matter in its wavelike state is said to be of the same nature as light. Tregear defines Tu as the name of "one of the greatest and most widely worshipped of Polynesian deities."[20]

According to the Dogon, matter exists in three conceptual *Worlds*. It begins in the perfectly ordered state of waves in the *First World*. An act of perception causes the waves to be disrupted and then to be fundamentally reordered in the *Second World*. This reorganizational process culminates in the egg-of-the-world, or po pilu, which is considered to be the first finished structure of matter. That egg then becomes the source of transformations that produce the *Third World,* which is defined as the familiar realm of our material universe. We consider the Dogon Second World of matter to be a conceptual correlate to the Egyptian Other World or Underworld, which is also known as the Tuat.

The Maori word *tua* also refers to "religious ceremonies taking place at the naming of a child,"[21] comparable to the modern-day Jewish tradition of a child-naming ceremony. Tregear roughly equates these ceremonies to a baptism, and so the suggestion is that there may be an underlying symbolic relationship to water. Appropriate to the intermediate nature of the creative processes of the Second World of matter, the Maori word *tuao* means "transient" or "not permanent."[22]

The suffix *tahi* of the word *tuatahi* also carries meanings that are understandable within the context of our cosmology. In the philosophies of various cultures, the processes that generate matter are dependent on the *feminine energy* associated with the nonmaterial universe that comes together with the *masculine energy* of the material universe. Appropriate to that outlook, the Maori word *tahi* implies the notion of "joining or meeting together."[23] The same word can also mean "to beckon to" or "to wave to," symbolism that is associated in other cultures with the concept of the Mother Goddess who creates matter.

An important aspect of Dogon village life centers on a structure called the *togu na* or *toguna,* defined as a "discussion house." Much of the day-to-day tranquility of Dogon life can be credited to concepts that are associated with this structure. It is a rule of a Dogon village that whenever a dispute arises between two or more tribe members, all interested parties are required to retire to the discussion house and are not allowed to leave until the dispute has been resolved. The toguna structure is built only to half-height, so that anyone who participates in discussions there will be obliged to sit, rather than stand. A likely Maori counterpart for the term *toguna* is formed from the words *tohu,* meaning "to think,"[24] and *nga,* meaning "to breathe."[25] The combined term can also be seen as a likely origin for the title of a wise, skilled, or priestly person, referred to as a *tohunga.*

Best assigns the word *tuarua* to the second stage of Te Kore. The Maori word *rua* means "two," and combined with the ordinal prefix *tua,* it means "second."[26] The Maori prefix *ru* means "to shake" and can imply a "rumbling sound," comparable to the Hebrew concept of *ruach.*[27] From a cosmological perspective, the symbolism indicated is the concept of *vibration,* an effect that is assigned to a primordial wave once it has been perceived. Consistent with these meanings, Tregear tells us that the Maori deity Ru was the god of earthquakes.[28]

An alternate meaning for the word *rua* is "by two and two," a meaning that seems to convey the notion of *duality,* which represents an underlying principle of the cosmology.[29] The phonetically similar

Egyptian word *ruu-t* means "separation," a second cosmological concept that, along with vibration, pertains to a perceived wave.[30]

The third Maori stage of Te Kore carries the name *tuatoru*. As we might now anticipate based on the pattern set by the prior Te Kore stages, the word *toru* means "three" and *tuatoru* means "third."[31] The word *toru* combines the cosmological phoneme *to*, which implies "the concept of growth," with the phoneme *ru*, which we have interpreted to refer to "the concept of vibration." Concepts relating to the growth of matter are expressed through a series of symbolic metaphors that are defined within the cosmology. One Dogon cosmological metaphor relates the stages of matter to the growth of a plant, and so the Maori term *to* means "to throw up a stalk."[32] Another metaphor relates to the creational theme of biological reproduction and is expressed in relation to the growth of a *womb*. Appropriate to that image, the associated Maori word *to* means "pregnant."[33]

According to Dogon definitions, after a *primordial wave* is perceived, it is drawn upward and then encircles to create an enclosed space that is compared to a bubble. The Dogon phoneme *to* provides us with meanings that relate sensibly to that process. One definition means "to arc," and another means "to be in the interior of," referring to the now-encircled and enclosed space.[34] Looked at from the Dogon perspective, the concept of a pregnant woman's expanding womb seems like a very good symbolic choice to represent these concepts.

As a brief aside from our discussion of Maori definitions, it seems appropriate to comment on a kind of parallelism that can be seen between those terms and the stages of the history of the civilizing of humanity. The Maori word for "one," *tahi*, combines the root *ta*, meaning "earth," with the term *hi*, meaning "to draw up." Lifting the civilized state of humanity upward was one stated purpose of the Dogon instructional tradition that we associate with the Gobekli Tepe site. The word *rua* is formed from the root *ru*, an Egyptian term that means "lion." Use of this term in association with the second creational stage supports the notion that the Sphinx might possibly be a remnant of an early attempt to establish agriculture in Egypt during the era that immediately followed Gobekli Tepe. The term *toru* is a close match for an ancient name *Taru*, which we associated with the early dynastic-era agricultural kingship in Egypt in *The Mystery of Skara Brae*.

The fourth Te Kore stage of the Maori is defined by the term *tuawha*, meaning "fourth." The Maori word *wha* means "four-sided" or "square."[35] In the symbolic language of the cosmology, a *square* represents the concept of a "space." Likewise, because our material universe is defined as the fourth of seven material universes, the geometric figure of a four-sided square understandably comes to represent it. Moreover, when we consider that our material universe is associated conceptually with a masculine energy, the number four also comes to be symbolic of the male gender in the reversed symbolism of later eras. That numeric designation aligns with Dogon symbolism, which assigns the number four to a male, the number three to a female, and the number seven to an individual. Taking that symbolism an additional step upward, if four is the number that associates with our material universe (defined in relation to masculine energy), then the number three might also be considered to be symbolic of the nonmaterial universe with its feminine energy. From that perspective, the two paired universes, taken together and associated with the number seven, would represent a conceptual correlate to an individual.

Another Maori word *wha* means "to be revealed," "to be disclosed," or "to be made known."[36] The implication here is that, based on our reality, which consists of four dimensions (height, width, length, and time), at the fourth stage of creation, the concept of space is developed and so causes the notion of existence to become perceptible. A similar meaning is conveyed by the Egyptian word *hau*, which refers to the enclosed space of a hall, temple, or palace.[37]

The fifth Te Kore stage is represented by the word *tuarima*, meaning "fifth." The word *rima* can also mean "hand," a definition that could sensibly relate to the five fingers on a typical hand.[38] From the perspective of Dogon cosmology, the egg-of-the-world, or po pilu, is conceptualized as seven progressive rays of a star that extend outward from a central point. At the fifth stage, the five emergent rays take on the appearance of a hand. In the symbolic language of the cosmology, a hand or arm represents the concept of a *force,* and so the suggestion is that at this stage, the first force (gravity) exists. The Maori phoneme *ri* is a likely correlate to the Egyptian phoneme *re* or *ra,* which on one level we take to represent the concept of *gravity,* as exemplified by the sun, which exerts the primary gravitational influence in our planetary system.

The sixth Te Kore stage is expressed by the word *tuaono,* meaning "sixth." The Maori word *ono* means "to jerk a body forward," while the word *onoi* means "to move."[39] The implication here is that of the observed effect of the *force of gravity,* which tugs on mass. Supportive of this outlook, the Dogon word *ono* means "to suck."[40]

The seventh stage of Te Kore is referred to as *tuawhitu,* or "seventh."[41] In Dogon cosmology, the starlike rays of the po pilu are considered to be complete after the appearance of the seventh ray. From that perspective, it makes sense that the Maori word *whetu* means "star."[42] In keeping with this, a familiar symbol for the Tuat, which is the likely Egyptian correlate to this Second World of matter, consists of a star inscribed within a circle.

The eighth stage of Te Kore carries the name *tuawaru,* meaning "eighth."[43] Again in Dogon cosmology, at the eighth stage of the creation of the po pilu, the seventh ray grows long enough to pierce the "egg," an event that is considered to be the "death" of the current "egg" but also initiates the growth of a new "egg." Appropriate to this outlook, the Maori word *waro* means "death."[44]

The name of the ninth stage of Te Kore is given as *tuaiwa,* meaning "ninth."[45] The Dogon consider the egg-of-the-world to be complete after eight conceptual stages; however, the full progression to a completed atom (*po*) involves additional stages. From the Dogon perspective, a series of completed "eggs" are said to link together like "pearls on a string" (Buddhism makes use of the same symbolic image) to form *membranes.* The Maori word *ewe* refers to the "afterbirth" and, according to Tregear, relates to "the membrane of the foetus."[46]

The tenth and final stage of Te Kore is given the name *tuangahuru,* or "tenth" (based on the Maori word *tingahuru,* meaning "ten").[47] The structure of the po pilu is alternately characterized by the spiral that can be drawn to inscribe the endpoints of the seven rays of increasing length. The suggestion in the cosmologies of the Dogon and a closely related African tribe called the Bambara is that the spiral of the po pilu enfolds *light* between the coils of its spiral, which are comprised of *mass.* From this perspective, the structure of the po pilu effectively facilitates an "embrace" between the nonmaterial and material universes. Like an air bubble submerged in water, when the egg is "pierced" by vibrations, it emits light. (It seems possible that this staged process is what causes light to be emitted in discrete packets called *photons.*) The Maori word *huru* refers to the emission of light, characterized as the glow of the sun just before it rises or the glow of a burning fire.

In the metaphoric language of Dogon cosmology, fundamental particles that compose matter are referred to as "seeds." The egg-of-the-world, or po pilu, which takes the form of a tiny spiraling vortex, can be thought of as the first of these "seeds." One Maori word for "seed" is given as *huri,*[48] which also means "to turn round," "to twist," or "to overturn."[49] This same concept of "overturning" is one of the symbolic references related to the po pilu.

In Dogon cosmology, the processes that create the po pilu in the Second World of matter culminate with the formation of the primary component of matter, called the *po,* in the Third World (our material world). The Dogon word *po* refers to a primary component of matter that would be comparable to an *atom* in astrophysics. The word also refers to the concept of *primordial time.* Genevieve Calame-Griaule, the anthropologist who compiled the Dogon dictionary, refers to the po as "the smallest grain." She writes that the po "plays a very important role in Dogon cosmology [as the] picture of the atom, from which the universe emerged."[50]

Best tells us that the Maori word *po* refers to an unseen, intangible, unknowable concept that underlies the heavenly bodies of the universe. He also says that, for the Maori, the word *po* connotes:

> The period of time prior to the existence of the universe.
> The period of labour of the Earth Mother.
> The period of time after death.
> The spirit-world or the underworld.[51]

Tregear defines the Maori word *po* to mean "the Cosmic Darkness out of which all forms of life and light were afterwards evolved or pro-created."[52] More generally, the Maori word *po* can be used to convey "the concept of *night*."

The cosmological concept of the po can also be seen reflected in the similar Egyptian phonetic root *pa*, which means "to exist," the word *pau*, meaning "primeval time," and the word *pau-t*, which refers to "stuff, matter, substance, the matter or material of which anything is made."[53]

5 Mythic Themes of Maori Cosmology

Based on what we have learned from our studies over the course of this series of books, the original concept of a mythic storyline seems to have survived in its most essential form among nonliterate groups like the Dogon tribe in Africa. This makes sense, since what must have started as an oral tradition in eras prior to written language would have continued within these cultures in its root form. However, key aspects of this form can also be seen to carry forward in the later myths of many ancient cultures. For many modern students of mythology, the primary frame of reference would be to the myths of classical Greece or Rome. From our perspective, these represent later forms whose focus was often on the acts and interpersonal relationships of mythic deities, which could take on many of the attributes of a modern-day soap opera.

By contrast, in Dogon society, the cosmological myths constituted a class of story that was told around the fireside at night and therefore presented in a forum that was not strictly limited to trusted initiates of the tradition but rather was also open to the broader populace of uninitiated tribe members. Almost by definition, the storylines of these myths included information that was only of a generalized nature and so would not have reflected inner mysteries of the esoteric tradition. Among the main purposes of these myths, as we understand them, was to familiarize the tribal group with basic cosmological themes, introduce major symbols of the tradition, and frame various cosmological elements and relationships in ways that would hopefully pique the interest of potential new initiates.

Although several mythic Dogon characters came to be defined within these myths, only the creator god Amma rose to the level of a deity in the modern sense of the word. Events within any given myth most often centered on the specific actions of an individual character, and not on the social interactions of a pantheon of gods and goddesses. In their stated context and based on the well-defined meanings of the words that comprise their names, each Dogon character can be interpreted to represent a stage or aspect of creation that is illustrated by the actions of that character in the myth. From this perspective, the mythic characters themselves can be said to have a mnemonic quality, much like other symbols of Dogon cosmology.

In *The Pale Fox*, French anthropologist Germaine Dieterlen flatly declares that there is no single mythic storyline that outlines the totality of Dogon cosmological thought. However, throughout their writings Griaule and Dieterlen relate numerous episodes as a way of illustrating the Dogon outlook on various aspects of their creation tradition. This illustrative aspect is the same essential function that is served by the body of Dogon cosmological drawings.

Consistent with this mnemonic approach, the ancient civilizing plan assigned creational symbolism to everyday tasks that a tribesperson would perform or associated those concepts with objects and animals that populated a person's daily life. Structured in this way, seemingly routine activities served to reinforce both the instructed concepts of the cosmology and various skills of the civilizing plan. Through this arrangement, the structures of society came to be self-reinforcing and so contributed both to retaining cosmological knowledge in its correct form and to the long-term stability of the tribal culture. It was this same type of cultural stability, resting on an arguably similar system of cosmology, that characterized ancient Egyptian life over the course of several thousands years.

Attainment of these goals implied that the symbolism of the cosmology might have to be tailored somewhat to accommodate the varied living environments of different tribal groups. So for continental-based cultures such as the ancient Egyptians or the Dogon, the concept of the emergence of *space* (expressed as *the separation of earth from sky*) was compared to *the raising up of a mountain.* For the Maori, who were an island-based culture, the corresponding comparison was to *the raising up of an island from the sea,* an image that would carry more pertinent meaning within their specific sphere of reference.

One frequent tool of daily life that seems to have taken on cosmological symbolism in many different cultures is that of a *basket.* Commonly seen in ancient cosmological art, the basket is depicted with a hemispheric handle attached to (from the perspective of a two-dimensional painting or carving) a square-shaped container. In cosmologies of the post-Neolithic era (starting circa 3000 BCE), circles and hemispheres were symbolic of the heavens ("above"), or the nonmaterial realm, while a square represented the earth ("below"), or the material realm. From this perspective, we could interpret the shape of a basket to represent the coming together of the two realms. The written form of an Egyptian word *bairi,* meaning "basket," upholds this outlook. Symbolically, the word reads "spiritual existence and existence material."[1] As the Dogon priests relate, teachers who are described as having been of a nonmaterial nature brought civilizing knowledge to humanity in ancient times. Maori mythology emphasizes similar themes in the context of tales in which the Earth God Tane is said to acquire "baskets of knowledge." A similar Samoan tale tells of a child who "ascends to the sun" and returns with "baskets of blessings."

One Dogon word for "basket" is *tadu,* a term that is phonetically comparable to the Maori word *taruke.* The Maori root *taru* refers to "grass" or "herbage,"[2] the materials from which a basket is typically woven. Calame-Griaule tells us that the Dogon word implies "the basket system of the world, and is a prototype of the Celestial Granary," a concept that is symbolized by the Dogon shrine that we view as a counterpart to the Buddhist stupa. She goes on to describe the basket as "the first model of the ark," referring to the egg-of-the-world on which Dogon cosmology bases its concepts of matter. She also sees cosmological symbolism in the circular and square geometric forms that comprise the basket, concepts that reflect conceptual reversal in certain contexts. Regarding the symbolism of the basket, she explains that "backward, it represents the sky (square background, image of the cardinal points) and earth (circular overture)."[3] (Conversely, in the archaic view circles were often associated with the sky and squares with the earth. In accordance with this same kind of reversal in symbolism, a Buddhist stupa squares its base and rises to rounded forms, while the Dogon granary squares its roof and rests on a round base.) A second Dogon word for "basket," given as *tomo,* can also mean "to inform" or "to educate."[4] Similarly, the Maori term *tomo* can refer to "a large basket."[5] An Egyptian word for "basket," *tena,* calls to mind the name of the god Tane, who, according to Maori myth, acquired knowledge in baskets.

As we move forward historically from the archaic era to more modern ancient times, symbolic elements that originally took a generalized form tended to become more stylized. For example, the eight Dogon ancestors, who are more often referred to by their ordinal sequence than by individual names, are likely correlates to the eight paired deities of the Egyptian Ennead or Ogdoad. Beyond association with specific honored family lines of Dogon society and association with particular civilizing skills, none of the Dogon ancestors becomes individualized within their mythic plotlines—not in the same way that ancestral deities such as Neith, Ra, Ptah, Thoth, or Anubis do in ancient Egyptian mythology. Rather, the Dogon most often treat the term *ancestor* as a symbolic construct, one that relates most sensibly to concepts of biological reproduction. Like other cosmological words, the term takes on meaning in a variety of different contexts. As matter emerges, a pair of Dogon ancestors is defined in relation to each quadrant of the circular egg-in-a-ball figure. This figure consists of a circle divided by two intersecting lines of axis. From the perspective of biological reproduction, ancestors take on a generational aspect that could relate sensibly to genetics. Similarly, within the constructs of Dogon civil life, each ancestor heads a family lineage and so plays a role in the structures of the society itself.

In culture after culture, we find that the contours of ancient cosmology are entwined with elements of an instructed civilizing plan. The skills that comprise this plan are the same ones that would be required to move a culture from a state of hunting and gathering to one of agriculture. In the view from which the Dogon priests explain their tradition, specific civilizing skills were defined as *instructed Words,* and each skill was associated with one of the eight mythical ancestors. Similarly, in the ancient Chinese tradition, a group of eight mythic emperors were credited with having brought these same civilizing skills. Within the Maori culture, we can see evidence of a comparable set of associations reflected in terms like *ranga,* meaning "to weave," which recalls the name of the deity Rangi, or in the word *papua,* meaning "seed," which is phonetically similar to the name of the goddess Papa. These homonyms suggest a correspondence within the Maori culture between civilizing skills and ancestral deities.

Because a single set of symbols was used in the Dogon culture to define at least three parallel themes of creation, the complexities of symbolism as it functions within the Dogon cosmological tradition starts to become somewhat unmanageable. One apparent solution to that difficulty lies with a series of four-stage Dogon metaphors that effectively allow us to group symbols into distinct categories. Overt reference is made in the Maori culture to the most familiar of these metaphors, which is defined in relation to primordial elements comparable to *water, fire, wind,* and *earth.* However, other cosmological metaphors of the Dogon are also similarly reflected in the Maori culture. For example, symbolic references in the Dogon tradition are associated on another level with categories of living creatures of the animal kingdom. These categories were meant to define ascending stages of creation. Insects represent concepts of *nonexistence* coming into *existence,* fish are associated with the reorganization of *waves* into *particles,* four-legged animals correlate to the *formation of space,* and birds symbolize *material creation, spiritual ascension, and knowledge.* Similarly, Best notes that Maori terms associated with the Earth God Tane take the form of names of birds.[6] In accordance with the metaphoric progression of symbolism, the ancestry as it is given in Maori myths shows an evolution of the bird-related concepts that begin with insects such as flies and smaller vermin. At the topmost level of the metaphor, Maori bird references play out comparably to Dogon and ancient Chinese references. Many of these relate to the mythical theme of the Mulberry Tree, a symbol that demonstrates parallelism to the Tree of Life concept that survives in many ancient cultures.[7] In the Maori culture, these symbolic animal references are framed in relation to Tane's stated responsibility to render the forest fertile.

From ancient Egypt, the symbolism of hieroglyphic words suggests to us that the *hawk* or *falcon,* which is an icon of the Egyptian god Horus (or Heru), at one time held a symbolic meaning. Meanwhile in accordance with other four-stage Dogon metaphors, the working of a symbol is often compared to that of a *seed* (which initiates growth, as in the stages of the growth of a plant) or a *sign* (which catalyzes the formation of a *Word*). For the Dogon, our material universe constitutes a kind of reflected form or image, one that presents only an illusory appearance. Hawks, which in ancient Egypt came to be associated with kingship, are also commonly found in the region of Orkney Island (a region we associate with the term *aaru*) and in the nearby Faroe Islands. One Maori term for "hawk" is *aahu.*[8] Another is *kahu,* a term that can also mean "to spring up," "to grow," or "to foster."[9] Appropriate to the Dogon definitions and creational metaphor, the Maori word *kahua* means "form or appearance," while the word *kahui* refers to a "herd or flock."

A stone woodworking tool called an *adze* played a significant symbolic role in the mythologies of the Dogon and of ancient Egypt. The adze was also adopted as a glyph shape within the Egyptian hieroglyphic language, where we interpret it to represent the force or process by which waves attain mass.[10] Cosmologically speaking, Dogon symbolism of the adze relates to the differentiation of matter in its wavelike state into the first four primordial elements of *water, fire, wind,* and *earth.* Dogon discussion of the adze effectively sets the stage to introduce one of the four-stage metaphors for classifying cosmological symbols. The adze also plays a noteworthy role in the mythology of the Maori, which is again given in relation to the notion of waves. Best relates that whenever rough waters were encountered at sea, an expert priest who was in possession of a stone adze could offer it, along with carefully intoned incantations, as a way to calm the sea, moving the tool as if to chop at the waves.[11]

6 Pre-Buddhist and Hindu Influences on Maori Religion

I n his book *The Aryan Maori,* Tregear makes the argument that the Maori culture was historically rooted in the same general regions of the Fertile Crescent, and perhaps India, as the archaic tradition we have been pursuing. In support of that view, Tregear presents a long list of Maori words whose meanings he assigns to Sanskrit roots. As might be expected, many of these words center on phonemes that also have symbolic significance within an ancient cosmology that we believe was passed down to some later cultures by way of ancient India. In part because of the relationship of Maori words to Sanskrit words that Tregear perceives, he interprets various Maori mythic and cosmological references as having originated with Buddhism. However, from our perspective, the suggestion is that the Maori culture, like that of the Dogon, may reflect archaic influences that actually predated Buddhism and so ultimately were also ancestral to it. Likely affirmation of this outlook lies with a circumstance that Tregear himself notes: the lack of reference in the Maori culture to virtually any of the later Buddhist deities.

Among the Maori parallels to Buddhism that Tregear mentions are mythic storylines that assign the formation of the universe to the rupturing of a *cosmogonic egg,* a theme that is broadly shared among the traditions we have studied. He also cites as evidence of Buddhist influences on the Maori certain artifacts excavated in New Zealand, such as a bell that carried an inscription written in the Tamil language. Although Tregear acknowledges that the Maori never actually adopted a Buddhist faith, in his view such artifacts imply the likely presence of Buddhist priests in New Zealand. Looked at in another way, Tregear's artifacts seem to only necessarily imply the influence of a pre-Buddhist cosmological tradition comparable to the one we have been pursuing as the likely parent to later traditions in India and Africa, which we also associate closely with the Tamil. Best cites parallels to Hinduism in the Maori culture but makes no outward claim for a direct relationship between the religion of the Maori and Buddhism. As a foundation for his presentation of the key elements of the Maori creation tradition, Best does devote extended discussion to the nature of religion in general and to common aspects of its expression among early cultures and tribal groups.

Knowing that the linguistics of the cosmological term *po* may relate phonetically and symbolically to the concept of *buddha* in India, that term, which in our view directly ties to Dogon cosmology, also seems our likeliest entry point to Buddhist parallels to the Maori creation tradition. It is understood that the Sanskrit term *Buddha* can refer to "the awakened one," one who is roused to the realities of the universe and of existence. This definition echoes a theme that is commonly referred to in myths of ancient India, Egypt, and elsewhere. It also takes its expression in the notion of a *sleeping goddess.* For many cultures, the physical form of this sleeping goddess seems to have governed the plan of early stone houses and burial chambers during (and just following) the Neolithic era of our tradition. Likewise, in the metaphors of many cultures, the cosmological processes that culminate in the formation of the *atom,* or po, begin with what is described as a *symbolic awakening.* From that perspective, the po (as a conceptual counterpart to the Buddha) would be an outgrowth of the one who is metaphorically awakened.

In Maori cosmology, these same processes by which matter conceptually "awakens" can be expressed as a series of progressive stages whose names rest on the prefix *po te,* a term that, phonetically speaking, falls midway between the Dogon word *po* and the Buddhist term *buddha,* linked by the common term *po.* As a compound of two cosmological phonemes that can be reversed, the concept of *po te* can alternately be expressed as *te po.* The eight transformative stages that produce the po constitute the Dogon egg-of-the-world, or po pilu, a structure that compares to the tiny bundle of eight wrapped-up dimensions (called the Calabi-Yau space) of string theory. Through these processes, matter in its wavelike state is transmuted into mass, and then into matter in its particle-like state. Cosmologically, the po pilu relates to the po in the same way that the Calabi-Yau space relates to an atom in modern astrophysics.

We have mentioned that in Dogon cosmology, a set of specific cosmological metaphors are defined as conceptual guides by which to organize and understand the processes of creation. Concepts that relate to these metaphors are often given in distinctly scientific terms. For example, one of these metaphors is expressed in relation to how a spoken *Word* forms from sound vibrations. Within the perspective of this metaphor, the terms *breath* and *wind* become symbolic glosses for the concept of *vibration,* the impulse by which *mass* and *matter* are produced. Another of the Dogon metaphors for creation is framed as stages in the *growth of a plant* and so is cast in relation to *seeds* that sprout and grow into *reeds.* Very similarly, Best explains that the staged processes that are defined by the term *po te* denote phases in the growth of the progeny of the Earth Mother, during which they acquire "form, breath of life, and growth."[1]

From one symbolic perspective, the Dogon compare the transformations that result in the po pilu to the actions of a *sieve,* the same essential concept that we have taken the Hindu god Siva to represent in previous volume of this series. (Foundation for this outlook is found in chapter 15 of *Point of Origin* and relates to the process by which particles are said to be differentiated from waves.) This symbolism makes better sense when we understand that the Dogon, after harvesting beans they have cultivated, preserve them by covering them with sand. At some later time when they want to make use of the beans, the Dogon employ a sieve to separate the beans from the sand. This scenario relates metaphorically to the process by which *particles of matter* emerge from *waves*. Within the mind-set of the cosmology, the concept of *mass* is equated with the term *earth* and can be represented by the phoneme *ta,* and so it seems sensible that the Maori term for "sieve" is *tatari.*[2] The Maori root word *tari* means "to carry" or "to bring."[3] Based on these definitions, the word *tatari* might be reasonably interpreted to mean "brings mass."

The stages of creation, which are conceptualized in Buddhism as the process by which *multiplicity* emerges from *unity,* take definition in the geometry by which a Buddhist stupa shrine is ritually aligned. The base plan of the stupa begins with a circle that is drawn around a central stick called a *gnomon.* Execution of this simple figure creates a working *sundial,* by which the hours of a day can be measured. However, with a few additional geometric steps, the structure also evokes a line oriented from east to west that can be plotted daily to track the apparent back-and-forth motions of the sun over the course of the year. The plotted figure brings visibility to the concepts of a *solstice* and an *equinox* and can be used to differentiate seasons and to measure the length of both a season and a year. A likely Maori link to this same set of concepts is found in their word for "season," which Tregear gives (appropriately) as *po.*[4] The concept of a *year* is defined by the Maori word *tau,*[5] a phonetic term that becomes significant when used as a prefix to other Maori cosmological words. Another word *tau* means "to turn away," suggesting the motion of the tiny vortex that is conceptually associated with the po pilu. The Maori word *tautau* refers to "a string or a cluster," two scientific concepts that pertain to the formation of the Calabi-Yau space and to matter.[6]

Over the course of our studies, we have come to regard the geometric method by which a stupa shrine is aligned to represent a signature of the tradition. By this we mean that any culture in which key aspects of that alignment process are evident is likely to have been influenced by the same ancient cosmological tradition. For example, during the era of 3000 BCE, it is evident that the plans of the earliest civic centers in ancient China were aligned according to this same geometric method. Furthermore, there is clear evidence that these Chinese cities grew up around sites that originally served as ancient ritual centers. The implication is that the cities had housed ritually aligned shrines comparable to a Buddhist stupa.

Within the symbolism of the cosmology, the center point of the shrine (which also seemingly came to define the center point of early civic centers) was interpreted on one level as representing a *navel*. In the mythology of India that defines the deities Siva and Sati, an Osiris-like tale is given in which the goddess Sati is killed, her body is dismembered, and its various parts fall to earth in the form of standing stones called *pithas*, whose locations came to define the placement of important ritual centers. Since these stones effectively defined the center point of alignment for the ritual shrines that came to stand on the sites, the pithas can also be said to represent *navels*. Reflections of this outlook are seen in a Maori word for "navel," which Tregear gives as *pito*.[7] Based on their relative positions and roles in the ancient mythology of India, we see Siva and Sati as likely counterparts to Osiris and Isis in ancient Egypt. Traditional researchers recognize symbolic associations between Isis and the star Sothis, or Sirius, in Egypt. A likely connection is seen here to a Dogon practice in which large stones are placed on a plateau to represent stars that are important to their cosmology, and so also by inference to the Egyptian placement of stone structures on the Giza plateau.

The cosmological concept of *ascension* is one that is central to the practice of Buddhism. According to the parallel creational themes of the cosmology, the term can be applied to the spiritual growth of a person, to the progressive stages by which matter is conceptually "raised up," and to a concept of ascension in the larger universe by which an ostensible gateway or door can be reached between our material universe and its ostensible nonmaterial paired universe. Discussed in the context of a more worldly frame, the concept of ascension can be expressed in terms of efforts by a person to reach the top of a mountain. In Buddhism, a central aspect of ascension is defined by the word *sakti,* a term that relates to a kind of spiritual energy that emanates from the region of a person's navel and rises upward. However, the phoneme *s* is not vocalized in Maori words, so no direct phonetic correlate can be offered for the Buddhist term *sakti.* However, Tregear defines a Maori term for "ascend" as *kake,*[8] a word that is arguably within the same phonetic ballpark as *sakti.* It means "to ascend," "to climb upward," and "to excel" or "to rise above others."

7 Echoes of Gobekli Tepe among the Maori

Although the focus of many of the books of this series has been on the era that begins at around 3000 BCE, the path of research leads us to believe that many of these traditions may have originated in the much earlier epoch of around 10,000 BCE. The circumstance by which we find pre-Buddhist references among the Maori, but in the absence of any overtly Buddhist deities, would seem to place the Maori creation tradition along this same general path of descent. If so, then our expectation would be that Maori cosmology came out of this same 10,000 BCE era, which implies that we should also find evidence of symbolism from that era among the Maori.

In *Point of Origin,* the view we put forth of Gobekli Tepe was that many of the symbolic elements exhibited at the site were likely to have been passed down to later cultures through the auspices of the earliest cultural groups in the region of Turkey, Iran, and India. Specifically, we see the same set of symbolic elements seen at Gobekli Tepe celebrated in the matriarchal Sakti Cult of India, a tradition whose origins are to be found to the north and west of India, in the same general vicinity as Gobekli Tepe.

As we explored possible relationships between Gobekli Tepe and the later traditions of Buddhism and ancient Egypt, one entry point to connecting evidence was found in the word *tepe.* Correlated word meanings support the idea that the Egyptian concept of a revered archaic First

Time, known as Zep Tepi, could refer to Gobekli Tepe. (Likewise, the Buddhist notion that civilizing knowledge was first passed to humanity at a mountaintop location called Vulture Peak was supported by prominent images of vultures carved on the mountaintop megaliths at Gobekli Tepe.) This and other evidence has led us to associate the word *tepe,* or *tepi,* with archaic concepts and practices that ancient cultures came to revere as restricted or sacred. In fact, it could be argued that the word *secret* itself derives from the notion of esoteric rituals and concepts that were deemed to be *sacred.*

The Maori term *tepe* provides a direct link to concepts of ritual through a word that Tregear gives as *whaka-tepe.* (*Whaka* means "to cause," and the root phoneme *wha* means "four," a number that refers symbolically to our material universe.) The meaning of the word *whaka-tepe* is "to do anything with regularity and without omission."[1] It can also mean "to perform completely." We see likely linkage to the same concepts through the phonetically similar word *tapu.* Tregear defines the Maori word *tapu* to mean "under restriction" or "prohibited."[2] Best explicitly relates the Maori concept of tapu to the perhaps more familiar African term of sacred tribal restriction, *taboo.* The term *tapu* centers on aspects of the Maori culture that were understood to be restricted to the domain of priests and that were therefore prohibited to everyday common tribespeople. For these purposes, tapu was understood to be inherent to a word, ritual act, place, or person. A Maori term for "to sanctify" is given by Tregear as *whaka-tapu.*[3] However, the quality of tapu could also come to be incidentally imbued in, or acquired by, a person or object through improper association with some other restricted object, place, or ritual, somewhat akin to the way that certain metal objects can become magnetized through exposure to electrical currents. For example, stories are told of Maori tribe members who happened across an ancestral burial ground that was considered to be tapu. A person in this circumstance would be kept in strict isolation from the rest of the tribe until such time as a priest could ritually remove the quality of tapu from him.

In regard to the Maori notion of tapu, Best writes in an article called "Maori Medical Lore":

> The violation of *tapu* includes any interference with *tapu* objects, persons or places. For instance, when a house has become *tapu* for some reason, and is deserted, it must not afterwards be entered or burned or interfered with in any way. Only a priest, or those under *tapu* for conveying a body, or exhumed bones, may trespass on a burial place, or caves where bones of the dead are placed. Should any one else so trespass, then those bones of the dead will turn upon the intruder and slay him, or afflict him grievously. That is to say, the gods will punish that person.[4]

The Maori word *tapu* is a likely correlate to the Dogon word *taba*, which means "to touch with the fingers of the hand."[5] Budge interprets a phonetically similar Egyptian hieroglyphic word *teba* to mean "finger," but the glyphs used to write the word may imply a reference to the actions of the fingers.[6] The relationship of the word to restricted cosmological knowledge likely comes from its resemblance to a second Dogon word *taba*, meaning "plateau,"[7] a priestly locale that bears associations with restricted knowledge in various ancient contexts. The meaning plays out in the Maori culture in connection with religiously restricted people or objects that, under complex conditions, are forbidden to be touched. In support of that view, Best writes of the Maori concept in his book *Tuhoe, the Children of the Mist:* "All matters or actions pertaining to death are extremely *tapu*. Those who touch, or bury, the bodies of the dead, or handle bones of the dead at the exhumation, are excessively *tapu*."[8]

If we allow the possibility that, as with the Egyptian word *tepi,* the phonetics of the word *tapu* links us back to the era of Gobekli Tepe, then there are also important aspects of the concept of tapu itself that tie us to the archaic matriarchal tradition that we associate with the Gobekli Tepe site. One Maori outlook characterizes the notion of tapu as referring to something that is deemed to be *ritually unclean.* This aspect is seen most evidently in the Maori view that menstruating women hold to the quality of tapu. As in many other cultures (including the Dogon and even some modern Orthodox Jewish sects), in ritual situations, menstruating women were carefully isolated from other tribe members and from ritually pure objects or places. In Orthodox Judaism, a menstruating woman is disallowed from entering the sanctuary as a way of preserving its purity. For the priestly Dogon tribe, each village features a "menstrual house" that is meant to isolate women from the tribe as a whole during menstruation. In other cases, contact with a menstruating woman was understood to actually remove the quality of tapu from a person or an object. The Maori word *tepepepe* refers to "clots of blood," a meaning that affirms a likely association to menstruation. We see this as reflective of an archaic matriarchal tradition whose emphasis was on fertility and whose origins we trace to the era of Gobekli Tepe.

Ancient concepts of tapu can be seen to be reflected even in the practices of some modern religions. For example, Best cites that over time for the Maori, some requirements have become simplified, saying that tapu restrictions on a person who has been in the presence of a dead body can now be removed simply if the person bathes prior to eating. A similar ritual applies to traditional modern-day Jews who have been to a cemetery for a funeral. They may be expected to wash their hands prior to entering the house of the deceased for an after-service meal.

In *Point of Origin,* we interpreted the symbolism of the Gobekli Tepe site in relation to an archaic view that the creative processes of matter result from a kind of conceptual embrace between a *feminine nonmaterial energy* and a *masculine material energy.* We argued that certain elements carved on the Gobekli Tepe pillars were meant to reflect that embrace symbolically. These include the pair of carved arms that emerge from the side of one pillar and whose hands wrap around its end in a somewhat less-than-huggable embrace. They also include enigmatic symbols that were carved in the form of the letter *H* and that apparently survived in the Masonic tradition along with explicit symbolism that defines the figure of an *H* as representing an embrace between *feminine and masculine energies*. Likewise, figures that reconcile the figure of a circle and a square, such as the three "handbag" figures seen on a Gobekli Tepe pillar, arguably symbolize this same embrace.

From this perspective, the megalithic stonework that comprised the pillars at Gobekli Tepe can be seen to have symbolized *matter*. In the cosmology of the Maori, the principal male and female deities who underlie the processes of creation are Rangi and Papa, a pairing in which Papa is cast in the role of the *feminine*. However, common usage of the term *papa* among the Maori to mean "father" is suggestive of the kinds of symbolic reversals we have noted for other later cultures of our tradition, which opens the door to speculation that the Maori term *papa* may have once represented the *masculine* form. Looked at in this way, it then makes sense that *papa* also refers to the concept of *stone* (which originally symbolized the *masculine material energy*), and in particular to a *flat stone*, such as one of the megalithic Gobekli Tepe pillars. In that same sense, the Maori term *papa* also relates to the concept of a door or gateway and so may be symbolized by a pillared arch.

In *The Mystery of Skara Brae*, we made the argument that the instructional sanctuaries we perceive to have existed both at Gobekli Tepe and on Orkney Island were cast life-sized, in the form of the encircling chambers of matter referred to in various cultures by the term *ark*, or *arq*. From this perspective, the structures at Gobekli Tepe bear a likely relationship to a Dogon cosmological drawing that is configured similarly to the Gobekli Tepe circled pillars and is referred to as "the figure of Ogo's ark." *Ogo* is the name of a character who plays the role of *light* in Dogon cosmological myths.

Also in *The Mystery of Skara Brae*, we related the term *ark* to the cosmological phoneme *ar*, which implies the notion of ascending upward. In our view, it forms the phonetic root of the archaic name for Orkney Island, Argat, a term that we interpreted to mean "ascending gateways of matter." We argued that megalithic structures on the island

Ogo's ark
(from Griaule and Dieterlen,
The Pale Fox, 213)

E

represent the ascending stages in which matter is said to "awaken." We cited a similar Egyptian term, *arq-hehtt,* a compound term that implies the notion of a "temple or sanctuary of the ark." A comparable Maori term, *ara,* means "to rise up" or "to awaken."[9]

It makes sense that instructed initiates of the tradition would come to relate personally to the notion of an ark, given its theoretic role as a sanctuary for the instruction of civilizing skills, which were framed in parallel to a system of cosmology. Tregear tells us that, in the Maori culture, the firstborn child in a family (male or female) was trained to become a priest and was referred to by the phonetically similar term *ariki.*[10]

Among the enigmatic mysteries that are presented to us by the megalithic site at Gobekli Tepe is the unusual circumstance of its careful burial, an event that is thought to have occurred within a thousand years of its initial construction. Researchers know based on the types and placement of materials used to fill the site that its burial was a deliberate choice and not simply the consequence of forces of nature. They credit the high state of preservation of the site to the simple fact of its careful burial thousands of years ago. Similarly, the notion of *covering a thing over* is one that plays an important role in the system of cosmology we are pursuing, perhaps most overtly with the notions of a *hidden god* that are found in many traditions, such as the Dogon creator god Amma or the Egyptian god Amen. The significance of the concept, as well as its likely pertinence to the Gobekli Tepe site, can be seen in the form of an Egyptian word that means "to cover over," which is also pronounced *arq.* From that perspective, the act of covering the Gobekli Tepe site effectively served to associate the site with its cosmological name and so preserved that association symbolically.

Similarly, in our studies of ancient Egyptian hieroglyphic words, we have seen that concepts that relate to the formation of the first tiny component of matter, the spiraling egg-of-the-world (or po pilu, as the Dogon call it), are also defined in relation to the concept of *covering over*. On one level, the hemisphere shape that we associate with the concept of mass or matter is described by the Dogon as Amma "closing himself up" after having "molded the world." Similarly, our traditional concepts of death and burial (associated in Egypt and among the Maori with an Underworld comparable to the Dogon Second World of matter) rest on the idea of covering over the deceased person. From these perspectives, covering a thing over is understood as an act of completion.

Commensurate with this outlook, the Maori word meaning "to cover" is *korama*.[11] Phonetically, the word is formed on the root *ko*, which refers to "a wooden instrument for digging," comparable to a spear. The notion of a spear or a tusk is one that relates symbolically to Ganesha and to the Dogon egg-of-the-world. The phoneme *ko* also pertains to the Maori word *kora*, meaning "small fragment" or "atom." The larger term *korama* combines this word *kora* with the phoneme *ama*, which is arguably the name of a creator-deity. The notion of the "atom of Amma" is one that would properly refer to the Dogon egg-of-the-world, which can be characterized as an ark, or an arq.

8 Maori and Tamil Word Correlations

The thesis on Maori heritage that is promoted in Tregear's 1885 book *The Aryan Maori* documents many links between Maori words and the Indo-European roots of the Sanskrit language, but it expressly denies any consequential relationship between the Maori and the non-Aryan indigenous cultures of India. Tregear's viewpoint goes against our outlook on the evolution of an ancient system of cosmology that likely originated in the region of the Fertile Crescent and descended in part through these same indigenous groups to later cultures in India, Africa, and Asia. This progression notably includes the Tamil in India, who preserve the traditions of the Sakti Cult and speak the Dravidian languages. Our outlook rests in part on the role that Tamil words can be seen to play in Dogon cosmology. However, Tregear writes, "The Dravirian [Dravidian] (aboriginal Indian) languages have only a few words resembling Maori, and these have been picked up by forty centuries of residence in a land where the Aryan is lord. The Dravirian languages have no more affinity for Maori than the Maori has for reptiles."[1]

If we presume Tregear's perspective to be a correct one, then any apparent Tamil word correlations that might be demonstrated in the Maori language would have been acquired through day-to-day contacts, but without the opportunities that would have been necessary to acquire the innermost concepts of an esoteric cosmology. So with this as our working premise, one direct approach to reconciling our outlook with Tregear's might be to consider the extent to which Maori words reflect *root concepts* of the archaic cosmology. In our view, these concepts represent *insider information* known only by trusted initiates of the tradition and not likely to be assimilated through everyday associations. Their presence among the Maori would imply a period of extended closeness that Tregear's viewpoint specifically disallows.

As we proceed with these prospective comparisons, it is important to keep in mind that, notwithstanding Tregear's Maori/Sanskrit word comparisons, significant differences in phonetic structure may have evolved between language groups of different cultures over time. We have seen this to be the case previously as we have compared words between language groups. Sensitivity to these types of phonetic differences allows us to arguably correlate the Dogon concept of the Sigi celebration with the Egyptian word *skhai,* which means "to celebrate," and the Dogon word *yala* with the Egyptian word *ahau.* From the outset, we understand that the Maori language does not offer direct equivalents to the English letters *L* or *S.* Knowing this to be true, we might reasonably expect some of the terms that we correlate based on shared meaning to be phonetically inexact. However, we also know that cosmological terms typically carry more than one meaning, so in cases where the phonetics of a Maori word might represent only an approximation of the correlated Tamil word form, it might still be possible to demonstrate agreement for secondary meanings of a given term based on the same phonetic equivalence and thereby validate the comparison.

In the mind-set of the archaic philosophies of the cosmology, the processes of creation are induced when the feminine energy of the nonmaterial universe (characterized as *light*) becomes entwined with the masculine energy of the material universe (characterized initially as *waves* or *water*). Within that context, a likely place to begin our Tamil and Maori word comparisons would be with the name of the Maori god Ao, whom we associate (based on his cosmological role) with the Hebrew light god Yah. This outlook is upheld by Maori passages presented by Best that bear strong resemblances to verbiage in the biblical Book of Genesis. As this initial stage of creation is related in Genesis, the world began in darkness, and the spirit of God was said to "move upon the face of the waters." Accordingly, the Maori word *ao* means "light,"[2] and *ea* means "to appear above water" or "to emerge."[3]

Linguistic references cited in *The Mystery of Skara Brae* suggest that a deity named El, whom we take to be a surrogate of or counterpart to Yah, was celebrated on Orkney Island in Northern Scotland. In our view, the deity is commemorated in the name of the Bay of Skaill (*skhai El,* or "celebrates El"). Appropriate to that interpretation, the Tamil word *el* also means "light." This outlook is supported by the relationship between a second Tamil word, *mai,* meaning "water," and a comparable Maori word, *maea,* which means "to emerge" or "to appear above water."[4]

Within the mind-set of the cosmology, this entwining of the feminine nonmaterial *essence* with masculine material *substance* is characterized as an *embrace*. It is the *feminine* or *matriarchal* aspect of this embrace that is emphasized in the archaic tradition and expresses itself within the Sakti Cult in relation to two Mother Goddesses whose names rest on the word *penu*. These goddesses are Dharni Penu and Tana Penu. In Tamil culture, the concept of "female" is expressed by the same phonetic root, *pen,* that is applied to nurturing Mother Goddesses. Although there appears to be no direct Maori phonetic equivalent to the Tamil word, the Maori word *penapena* carries the motherly meanings of "to cherish, to foster, to take care of."[5] Meanwhile, the Tamil word for "male" is given as *an,* very much as the Maori word for "male" is *ana*.[6]

From the perspectives of both the Dogon priests and modern astrophysicists, an act of *perception* causes matter in its wavelike state to behave like particles. The Dogon say that the act of perception disrupts the wave, causes it to *vibrate* and *pivot,* and thereby induces changes in the physical state of the wave. These changes are described as *phase transitions,* which are comparable to the transformation that occurs in water as cold temperatures transmute it into ice. The Tamil word for "embrace" is *taluvi*. The comparable Maori term (which may express the sound of the Tamil *L* as an *H*) is *tahu,* meaning "spouse." Suggestively, however, the word *tahu* also means "to kindle," and it is the phonetic root of the word *tahuri,* which means "to turn around" (pivot) or "to set to work."[7] The underlying Tamil root *ta* means "to give, grant, or bestow," while the Maori root *ta* means "belonging to."[8] Our choice to correlate the Tamil phoneme *tal* with the Maori phoneme *tah* is supported by an additional pairing between the Tamil word *talai,* meaning "head," and another Maori word *tahuri,* which also means "head."[9]

In the symbolic language of the cosmology, the notion of *vibration* can be characterized as *wind* or as *breath.* Similarly, within the Tamil language the concept of "breath" is expressed by the word *ha.* For the Maori, the comparable term *whaka-ha* means "breathe."[10] The Maori prefix *whaka* means "to cause" or "to cause to."[11]

One important storyline that serves as a common metaphor for the seven stages of creation of the "egg" of matter is that of the cross-cultural myth of the Seven Houses. Varying renditions of this myth, which are given both in India and in Egypt, compare the emergence of matter to an *awakening.* From this perspective, Yah's commandment "let there be light" is reflected in the act of a sleeping woman (or goddess) who simply opens her eyes as she awakens to the light of a new dawn. From this perspective, Yah represents the glow of light from a rising sun that comes to define the shapes that she perceives. In many of the traditions we have studied, concepts that pertain to light are expressed using the phonemes *ak, akh,* or *aakhu* (the Dogon *ogo*). In keeping with that outlook, the Tamil word *aku* means "to become," while the comparable Maori word *ahu* means "to cultivate," "to foster," or "to heap up."[12] Similarly, the Tamil word *akaram* means "shape," while the Maori terms *ahua* and *kahua* also mean "shape."[13]

From the Dogon perspective, the processes of creation culminate in the first coherent structure of matter, which is referred to as the *po pilu.* One entry point for our cosmological comparisons to the Maori rests on concepts they share in common with the Dogon regarding the nature and symbolism of the atom-like po. The cosmological terms *pil, pille,* and *pilu* serve as a connecting link for cosmological concepts among a number of ancient cultures, and various meanings of the terms play out in relation to symbolism of the elephant god Ganesha in India. Ganesha was seen as the son of a mother goddess and was given the head of a white elephant. Appropriately, depending on the language involved the word *pilu* can mean "elephant," "son," or "white." The po pilu itself is seen as a bubble-like structure that is associated with seven arrow-like or spear-like rays of a star, the last of which grows long enough to finally pierce and burst the bubble. In this context, it is understandable that the Tamil word *pil* means "to burst" and is a term for "arrow." The arrow is also a traditional icon of various goddesses who can be seen as surrogates to Ganesha's mother. A comparable Maori word, *pahu,* also means "to burst,"[14] while the word *pere* means "arrow."[15] Similarly, the Tamil word *po* means "perforate" or "to make a hole," while the Maori word *poaha* means "open."[16]

From the metaphoric viewpoint in which the action of the chambers of the po pilu is compared to that of a sieve, Ganesha is conceptualized as the keeper of the gateways that divide the chambers. As such, he comes to be associated with the placement and removal of obstacles. In keeping with this outlook, the Tamil word *tatai* refers to an "obstacle," while the Maori word *tatari* means "strainer, sieve," or "to strain or sift."[17]

We have discussed the obvious correlations that can be shown to exist between the Maori concept of the po and the Dogon po, most specifically as a conceptual correlate to a scientific atom. These terms are also reflective of concepts as they are expressed in the Tamil language, where the notions of "substance" and "material" are expressed as *porul.*

Several other aspects of the ancient system of cosmology can be seen to be reflected in word forms that are shared commonly by the languages of the Tamil and the Maori. Both the Dogon and Buddhist traditions take their symbolic forms in relation to an aligned ritual shrine that the Buddhists call a stupa. The geometric plan of the shrine replicates the stages of creation by which matter comes to be established and grow. The stupa form is a conceptual correlate to the steeple of a church. In keeping with these definitions, the Tamil word *stupi* refers to the "top of a temple," and the Maori word *tupu* means "growth" and implies the notion of being "firmly rooted" or "firm."[18]

Another symbolic concept that has importance for the cosmological tradition is that of an *ancestor*. This same concept arguably lies at the heart of the Maori outlook that conceptualizes the processes of creation in relation to genealogies. We have said that in the mind-set of many ancient traditions, an ancestor was conceptualized as having preceded you and so would stand "before" or "ahead of" you. From that perspective, the Tamil word *mu* expresses the notion of "that which was before," while the Maori words *mu* and *mua* refer to an "ancestor" and to "the front or forepart" of something.[19]

Finally, in the Dogon and Egyptian traditions, the concept of "completion" is expressed by the words *toymu* and *temau,* while in many ancient traditions the phoneme *mu* can be seen to refer to *water.* Likewise, in many traditions the birthing process is brought to completion with a ritual baptism. Similarly, the Tamil word *toy* means "to dip in water," while the phonetically similar Maori word *tohi* refers to a "baptismal ceremony."[20]

Cosmologically speaking, we see a great deal of overlap among cosmological concepts of the Maori, the Dogon, and the Tamil that are supported by cosmological words of the Maori and the Dogon. That observation goes against Tregear's perception that no significant relationship could be demonstrated between Tamil words and Maori words. Meanwhile, it is consistent with his report of the finding of an ancient bell in New Zealand with Tamil words inscribed on it. Based on all of this, a reasonable person could easily conclude that we do, in fact, see Tamil influences in the Maori culture.

9 Evidence of the Sakti Cult in Maori Culture

Our outlook on the archaic cosmological symbolism of Gobekli Tepe is that one primary path of its transmission to later cultures was through the Sakti Cult in India. The Sakti Cult is thought to have originated in regions nearby the Fertile Crescent and is traditionally seen as a direct predecessor of the later Vedic, Buddhist, and Hindu religions. Key cosmological concepts of the Sakti Cult are evident among the Tamil and are expressed in the words of their language, much as the existence of similar concepts can be demonstrated in the modern Turkish language. While key words of Dogon cosmology are demonstrably ancient Egyptian words, the Dogon language is understood to consist of discrete subsets of words from several different language groups. Many of these same concepts are also evident in the Dogon culture, where they are also given in relation to Tamil or Turkish roots. Because the modern Dogon culture seems to closely reflect the civic and cosmological practices of ancient Egypt at around 3000 BCE, the suggestion is that the same elements may have also influenced predynastic culture in ancient Egypt. Evidence from predynastic locales such as Elephantine, Saqqara, and the ancient stone quarry of Gebel el-Silsila supports this outlook.

We have said that, in its earliest forms, the archaic tradition that seems to underlie these cultures was a matriarchal one, with emphasis on Mother Goddesses such as the two sister goddesses, Dharni Penu and

Tana Penu, of the Sakti Cult and later goddesses of India such as Sati and Devi. Also pivotal to the cosmological symbolism of these traditions was the elephant-headed god Ganesha, who was the son of the two sister goddesses, or according to alternate myths, of Sati. Various icons and symbolic attributes of Ganesha have significance outside of India in such cultures as the Dogon and ancient Egypt, despite the absence in those groups of surviving references to an elephant god. The suggestion is that early cosmological elements were passed along from India to these cultures, but such passage may have preceded later personification of those meanings in the form of anthropomorphized deities.

On first impulse, the two sister goddesses of the Sakti Cult may call to mind the sisters of Isis and Nephthys in ancient Egypt. The goddess Isis was understood to symbolize Sothis, the bright star of Sirius. The Dogon understand that this main sunlike star of Sirius has a dark dwarf star companion, which we see represented in Egypt by Isis's dark sister, Nephthys. Similarly, one of the sister goddesses of the Sakti Cult was named Dharni Penu (the word *dharni* means "luminous," perhaps distantly similar to a Maori term *puhana,* which means "glowing"), and the other was an Earth Mother goddess named Tana Penu. Cosmologically speaking, the term *earth* implies the concept of "mass," which is a key attribute of a dwarf star. So like Isis and Nephthys, we interpret the two Sakta goddesses to have symbolized the same two binary stars of Sirius. (Note that as a general usage, Sakti Cult goddesses are often referred to as Sakta goddesses.) In terms of a general outlook, the Sakti Cult does not fall very far from the main premise of Maori cosmology, which is that all natural phenomena descended from a Sky God or Sky Parent and an Earth Mother. Best himself cites comparisons to Hinduism as a correlate when characterizing Maori cosmological principles.[1]

Allowing for reversals in symbolism that seem to have been instrumental in transforming the matriarchy of the archaic era into a later patriarchy, it is understandable that the likely correlate of Tana Penu in Maori cosmology might be not a mother goddess named Tana, but rather a creator god named Tane. Tregear defines Tane as "one of the greatest divinities of Polynesia. He was known and worshipped in almost every island of the Pacific, either as the male principle in Nature, or as the god of Light."[2] Best echoes Tregear's definition when he flatly asserts, "We may state briefly that Tane represents the male principle generally."[3] Knowing that on one level of interpretation the Sakta goddesses stood as representations of the female principle, we can see that Best's understanding of the cosmological significance of Tane constitutes a very direct reversal of that same symbolism.

Maori references indicate that there were relationships between Tane and several of the aniconic elements that traditionally defined the Earth Mother goddess Tana Penu in the Sakti tradition. Best tells us that mythic storylines define Tane as having married the Mountain Maid, and so like Tana Penu, he comes to be closely associated with mountains. Cosmologically speaking, during the processes by which matter forms, *mass* (defined as "earth") is said to be drawn up in the shape of a mountain. Parallels to the Sakta goddesses can also be seen in Tane's association with *standing stones*. Best tells us that "certain upright stones were known as the 'stones of Tane'"[4] and that these stones served as altars and places where family offerings were made. Best mentions that the stones were sprinkled with water, a detail that calls to mind the clay pots filled with water (called *potbellies*) that were associated with Tana Penu.

Although it seems an unlikely role to be assigned to a male god, Tane was also responsible for certain fertility rituals, which is comparable to the fertility symbolism that characterizes Tana Penu. For example, it was Tane who was responsible for preparing "the Living Water in which the moon renews herself every month."[5] This responsibility, which should more intuitively fall to a Mother Goddess, serves as further evidence of the theoretic reversals in symbolism that we believe to have occurred in later eras of the cosmological tradition. The Maori concept of the Living Water, referred to as *Waiora* or *Te-Wairoa-a-Tane,* is one that is rooted in fundamental outlooks on the nature of our universe as they are given in the cosmology we have been pursuing, which postulate the existence of a primordial source for creation that is of the nature of waves or water. As is true for the archaic cosmology, Polynesian traditions associate these waters with the Tree of Life. The Maori notion is that the Living Waters are located in the *fourth heaven,* the source from which the soul of a new baby is drawn.[6] From the perspective of the Dogon cosmological tradition, ours is the fourth of seven material universes.

In discussions of Tane's relationship to another Maori deity, Tiki, Best himself cites examples of reversals in the gender role for Tiki that appear in Maori lore, some of which cast him in a biological role comparable to a *phallus,* while others overtly state that Tiki was given by Tane as a wife for Io. These discrepancies call to mind similar ambiguities of gender that have come to exist within Dogon cosmology in relation to their creator god Amma. In India, the word *amma* can be traced to Sati, who was the mother of Ganesha. There, *amma* is an affectionate term by which Ganesha refers to his mother, Sati, akin to *mommy.* Griaule quotes the Dogon priests as referring to their creator god Amma as being both male and female. This outlook might be seen to uphold a principle of dual opposites in Dogon cosmology, or it might possibly represent the accommodated result of a historical reversal in symbolism.

10 Symbolic Aspects of Ganesha in Maori Cosmology

In *Point of Origin,* we devoted an entire chapter to the discussion of the cosmological symbolism of eight classic incarnations of Ganesha. We referenced a well-known article called "Ganeśa as Metaphor: The *Mudgala Purāna,*" by Phyllis Granoff of Yale University, whose outlook was that the incarnations represent progressive stages of creation. We argued that this symbolism becomes understandable when it is examined within the context of Dogon discussions of the egg-of-the-world and the processes by which matter forms. The symbolic meanings of various ancient terms used to describe these incarnations are made even more obvious when we interpret them in relation to various correlated words of Dogon and ancient Egyptian cosmologies. However, many of the meanings are also evident in the Tamil and Turkish languages and therefore (given what we see as the likely history of transmission) take on the appearance of representing original information of the tradition, as opposed to later developments. Looked at from this perspective, any later culture such as the Maori who may have emerged from this same tradition also might reasonably have knowledge of key aspects of it.

Our correlations to Ganesha were made in relation to Dogon cosmological drawings of their egg-of-the-world, which include a series of starlike rayed figures enclosed within an oval egg. Essentially, rays of

increasing length are added at each new phase of generation of the egg
and are shown as emitting from a central point. This progression evokes
a figure with seven rayed lines that is interpreted by the Dogon priests
from several perspectives. Outwardly, the figure is seen as a seven-rayed
star or characterized by the spiral that can be drawn to inscribe its rays.
But by one alternate interpretive approach, the rays are considered in
two groups, one of four lines that are symbolic in Dogon numerology
of the *feminine*, and one of three lines, considered to be *masculine.*
Numerologically, the combined total of seven rays represents the concept of an *individual.* By a second approach, the rays are grouped to
form two anthropomorphized stick figures whose configurations reflect
the two most common representations of Ganesha—one with two
arms, two legs, and a single tusk, and one with four arms who dances
on a single leg. In accordance with the Dogon numerology, the Maori
term for "four" is *wha,* and the phonetically similar term for "female"
is *wahine.*[1] The Maori word for "three" is *toru,*[2] while the phonetically
similar word for "male" is *tourawhi.*[3]

In India, the elephant god Ganesha was assigned the role of *gatekeeper* by his mother Sati, to watch the door while she bathed. One of
his celebrated roles in the religious traditions of India was to impose or
remove obstacles for individuals, in proportion to the degree of their
spiritual worthiness. The word *pil,* or *pilu,* can mean "elephant" in the
various languages of the traditions we study, and from that perspective, the spiraling structures of the po pilu can be seen as the *po of the
elephant,* a term that implies Ganesha. Appropriate to all of that, the
Maori term *pokai* means "to wind in a ball, as string."[4]

From a cosmological perspective, the suggestion is that Ganesha
represented the gateways between the wrapped dimensions of the
Calabi-Yau space. The Egyptian term we correlate for the structures and
gateways that comprise the po pilu is *arit.* So it also makes sense that a
Maori term for "obstacle" is given as *aria.*[5] Likewise, one of the signature icons of Ganesha is his single tusk. Tregear lists a Maori word for
"tusk" as *rei.*[6] Within one cosmological view, each stage of the egg-of-

the-world can be characterized as a *ray* of a star, or by way of metaphor as a *tusk.*

In Hindu mythology, Ganesha was described as the son whom Sati created from clay and whom she then breathed life into. Through a misunderstanding of circumstance, Ganesha was beheaded by the god Siva, who (after realizing his mistake) made great effort to procure a new head for Ganesha. It was taken by permission from a wise, aging white elephant, who, being near to death anyway, agreed to donate it. In keeping with these mythic references, the words *pil, pilu,* or *fil* carry the meanings of "elephant," "son," or "white" in various ancient languages. For the Maori, the term for "white" is pronounced *taurei,* a word whose phonetics aligns well with *arei* ("obstacle") and *rei* ("tusk").[7] However, the word *taurei* can also mean "pale." This is a Dogon cosmological term that is closely associated with the formation of matter. In fact, the definitive French study of Dogon cosmology is titled *Le Renard Pale,* or *The Pale Fox.*

Myths of India that relate the origin of the elephant god Ganesha tell of how the goddess Sati yearned for a son, and so while her husband Siva was away, she fashioned one from clay and then breathed life into him. These plot details serve to align Sati (through symbolic gender reversal) with the Maori war god Tu, since Best tells us that "Tu made a clay image in human form and endowed it with the breath of life, by the grace of his own magic powers."[8] Once again, turning to the Maori dictionary, we find that Tregear defines Tu as "one of the greatest and most widely worshipped Polynesian deities."[9] Just as the Sakta goddess Tana Penu (of whom we take Sati to be a surrogate) had a twin sister Dharni Penu, Tu was also understood by some versions of Maori myth to have had a twin brother. This detail again makes sense based on our outlook of symbolic reversals in the cosmological tradition.

Tregear explains that one of Tu's foremost titles was Tu-Mata-Uenga. The Maori word *mata* means "face,"[10] and the term *uanga* refers to "a time or circumstance [period?] of raining" or flooding.[11] The combined terms come remarkably close to expressing the biblical notion of "the face of the waters" that, in the view of some traditions we study, represents a starting point for the processes of creation.

We have said that one of Ganesha's traditional roles in Hinduism is as the imposer and remover of obstacles. This role is made clearer when we consider that the processes of the Dogon egg are compared to that of a sieve (which also likely defined the symbolism of the Hindu god Siva). A sieve represents a set of obstacles that allows us to productively separate two unlike materials from one another. Cosmologically speaking, the Dogon egg works like a sieve in that it effectively separates *particles* from *waves*. For the Maori, the concept of a sieve is expressed by the word *tatari*.[12] The phonetic roots of the word, *ta* and *tari,* demonstrate a likely match to Dogon and Egyptian concepts of matter, where the word *ta* implies the notion of "mass." One generalized outlook on matter that the Dogon and Egyptian cosmologies share with modern string theory is that matter is the product of woven threads. In keeping with that notion, the Maori word *tari* refers to "a mode of plaiting," which is a method of braiding or weaving various strands of a material.[13] The word can also mean a "noose," a tool that is woven from rope (bundles of threads) and that is one of the iconic cult objects of Ganesha. Furthermore, we know that, in the symbolic language of the cosmology, the phoneme *ta* refers to the concepts of "mass" or "matter." The Maori word *tari* can also mean "to carry." Together, they express the combined concept of "to carry or bring mass," one of the overtly defined functions of the egg-of-the-world. We have also mentioned that on another level of Dogon interpretation, the processes of matter are compared to the workings of an adze, a woodworking tool similar to a planer that can be used to shave wood. Consistent with that metaphor, the Maori term *tarei* means "to adze."[14]

A likely Maori correlate to Ganesha lies with a deity named Rehua. Tregear defines Rehua as "one of the most powerful and ancient Maori deities: the Lord of Kindness, who dispersed gloom and sorrow from the minds of men."[15] Support for the supposition that the Maori god Rehua bears a likely symbolic relationship to Ganesha can be found by examining Maori words for various iconic attributes of the elephant god. Many of the meanings center on the previously discussed roots *re* and *rei,* which we take to form the phonetic basis of the name *Rehua.* For example, we know that Ganesha was associated with the concept of a *single tusk,* and in *Point of Origin* we used specific comparisons to Dogon cosmology to demonstrate a likely origin for that symbolic assignment. (In our view, it derives from a kind of stick-figure interpretation of the seven rays of the Dogon egg-of-the-world, in which the final ray is interpreted as a tusk.) We have also mentioned previously that the Maori word for "tusk" is *rei.*[16] Likewise, because Ganesha's original head was said to have been replaced with the head of an aging white elephant, the color white becomes a symbolic term that relates to him. The color assignment comes to him by association with the Sakti tradition, where white (a color that conceptually subsumes all other colors of the spectrum) is taken to be symbolic of the divine. The Maori word for "white" is *tuarei.*[17]

We have said that, in his role as the cosmological gatekeeper, Ganesha is seen as the imposer and remover of *obstacles.* The Maori word for "obstacle" is *arai.*[18] One of the iconic objects Ganesha is seen to be holding in images and sculptures is a noose. The Maori word for "noose" is *rore.*[19] One possible clue to the symbolism of the noose is found in the phonetically similar Maori word *rorerore,* which means "entangled." *Quantum entanglement* is a term of modern-day astrophysics that applies to pairs of electrons whose quantum states seem to become inherently linked to one another.

From the perspective of the archaic tradition of the cosmology, we have noted that certain complex phonemes are reflected in important cosmological words. For example, the archaic Egyptian term *get* was interpreted by Budge for later Egyptian words as *het.* We surmised that the prefix of the name of an archaic Egyptian sanctuary, given as *Ga nu sa Ast,* survived in India as *Ganesha.* We interpreted the phonetics that defines the first three stages of the Dogon egg-of-the-world as *ga, nu,* and *sa.* These stages are the product of vibrations of matter that are referred to symbolically as *breath*. So it could make sense that the Maori word *ha* means "breath."[20] The related term *hanene* means "blowing softly" or can refer to a "soft breeze." The term *haha* means "to ward off," a definition that might conceivably go along with Ganesha's role of creating obstacles. Like his theoretic Egyptian surrogate god Hapy, Ganesha was seen as a god of abundance. Perhaps appropriate to that definition, the Maori term *hanu* refers to "scraps of food." This definition is given within the context of "gathering things together that are thinly scattered," a process that could characterize what the egg-of-the-world or Calabi-Yau space accomplishes for mass. Similarly, the Maori term *hari,* meaning "to dance," reflects another iconic aspect of Ganesha, arguably combining the phonemes of *ha* and *rei.*

11 Ancient Egyptian Word Correlations to the Maori

If our intent was to try to synchronize the Maori and Egyptian outlooks on their respective cosmologies, the place to begin might be with the Maori concept of tapu, which we have noted that Tregear defines to mean "under restriction" or "prohibited."[1] Again, the Maori term *tapu* properly applies to all restricted or esoteric knowledge and practices. This is arguably the same body of knowledge that, as Griaule described in his book *Conversations with Ogotemmeli*, Dogon priests took such care to reveal only to trusted initiates. The Dogon word *ta* can mean "gate" or "doorway,"[2] and the word *pu* refers to the concept of "totality."[3] Taken together, the Dogon term *tapu* would refer to a body of knowledge that might be seen as "the gateway to totality," the same knowledge that was restricted to trusted initiates. From an Egyptian perspective, and knowing that the precise pronunciations of Egyptian words are uncertain, we see a likely reference to this same body of restricted knowledge reflected in the ancient Egyptian term *tepa,* which Budge defines to mean "to overstep" or "to transgress."[4]

By way of a few examples cited so far in the preceding chapters, we can see that likely relationships exist between some Maori and ancient Egyptian words of cosmology. Likewise, if our Te Kore comparisons suggest that the Maori and Dogon cosmologies align, and we know that we have already correlated many of the Dogon cosmological words and concepts to ancient Egyptian words, then by a kind of transitive property of cosmology and language we can reasonably presume that parallels will be found between some words of Maori cosmology and ancient Egyptian words. However, there are a number of key Maori terms that very obviously seem to express ancient Egyptian concepts, and so it makes sense to review a few of these.

Perhaps the most recognizable of these words begin with the name of the Egyptian sun god Ra. Tregear tells us that the Maori word *ra* refers to "the sun, the name of the solar deity." It's fair to say that during the dynastic era, Ra was the premier god of Egyptian culture. In fact, our outlook is that one of the ancient names for Egypt, *Mera,* can be interpreted to mean "loves Ra." Similarly, Tregear goes on to say that this Maori deity Ra "was known by this name almost everywhere in Polynesia."[5] He adds that in New Zealand, although no deity can be said to have been overtly worshipped, great respect was paid to the beneficial attributes of the sun, which were also assigned to the term *ra.*

From a cosmological perspective, Ra aligns symbolically with the notion of the *bending and warping of mass* that is associated with the force of *gravity.* Within the purview of our immediate solar system, the sun is the prime generator of gravity, whose tug keeps the other bodies of the solar system in their orbits, and so Ra might well have come to be symbolic of that concept. In keeping with this outlook, the Maori word *rahu* means "to gather" or "pull about."[6]

Obvious similarities can be seen between the Maori Earth Mother Papa and an Egyptian word *papa,* meaning "to bring forth," "to bear," or "to give birth to."[7] Symbolic links to the cosmological notion of the emergence of space can be seen in the glyphs of the word, which are expressed with the *square glyph* □ (the square can represent the *material universe* and, by its form, illustrates the concept of "a space") and the *bent arm glyph* ⎯⎯⏌, meaning "to give," "to cause," or "to measure out."

The Egyptian concept of *light is* often given in relation to the phonetic roots *ak* and *akh.* From the perspective of the ancient cosmological tradition, matter begins as a kind of collected pool of primordial waves, from which matter grows in a manner that is compared meta-phorically to the growth of a *tree,* known as the Tree of Life. These waves are associated with the nonmaterial universe and are said to be of a nature that is similar to *light.* Consistent with that perspective, the Maori word *akar* means "root, origin, principle or foundation," and the word *akaaka* can refer to "the rays of the sun; the tree of life rooted in heaven above; the root of all existence; a spirit located at the very lowest point of the universe and sustaining the creation."[8]

In the Egyptian and Dogon languages, the concept of *water* or *waves* was conveyed by the term *nu.* This meaning is emphasized by the Egyptian term *nun,* which was assigned to the deified concept of the *primeval waters.* We can see evidence of the same phonetic symbolism in the Maori term *honu,* which means "fresh water."[9] The prefix *ho* in the Maori language implies the notion of a gift that is given, and so the suggestion is that the term for "fresh water" implies the only type of water that would be suitable to bring to someone for drinking, perhaps to be contrasted with salt water. It may also be cosmologically signifi-cant that the Hawaiian counterpart to the biblical character Noah, who is also associated with a great flood, was called Nuu.[10]

From both a scientific and an ancient cosmological standpoint, the processes that transform matter in its wavelike form into particles are initiated by an act of perception. The Egyptian term that defines this act is pronounced *maa* and means "to see, to examine, to inspect."[11] Various hieroglyphic spellings for the word include the Egyptian *eye glyph* . The word *maa* provides a phonetic root for the word *maa-t,* meaning "sight." A comparable Maori word is pronounced *mata* and means "eye."[12] The Maori word *ahi* refers to the concept of "fire."[13] This may correspond to an Egyptian word for "fire" that is given by Budge as *aaa,* pronounced roughly as *ahay* or *ayah.*[14] From the perspective of our comparative studies, *fire* can represent the act of perception that initi-ates the processes of the creation of matter.

The Maori word *ka* means "transformation" and is used "to denote one action changing into another."[15] The word is a likely correlate to the

Dogon phoneme *ke,* which, like the Egyptian word *kheper,* referred to a "dung beetle." From a cosmological perspective, the dung beetle represents the concept of *nonexistence coming into existence,* and its name relates to an Egyptian word *kheperu* that means "transformation."[16] In our view, an Egyptian glyph that is pronounced *ka* ⎵ is meant to depict the image of an *embrace,* comparable to the conceptual embrace that occurs between the nonmaterial and material universes when the processes of the creation of matter are catalyzed.

The Egyptian word *ar* means "to go up" or to "ascend" and can imply the concept of a staircase.[17] In our view, the same phoneme *ar* was reflected in the ancient name *Argat* for Orkney Island in Northern Scotland, where a series of megalithic structures was erected that appears to symbolize a series of ascending stages of matter. We interpreted the name *Argat* to refer to the "ascending gateways" of matter. In the myths of various cultures, these ascending stages of matter are symbolically associated with the notion of *waking up,* in much the same way that the modern act of waking up is commonly referred to as "rising." By comparison, the Maori word *ara* means "to rise," "to rise up," or "to awake."[18]

The Maori word *ara* also refers to "a road, a path, a way." The progressive stages of matter are characterized in the traditions of various cultures like the ancient Chinese as a *road, way, or path.* The Chinese word *dao,* which forms the phonetic root of the religion of Daoism, carries these same meanings, and likely correlates exist in the ancient Egyptian language. On Orkney Island, the megalithic structures that we interpret to represent progressive stages of matter were linked to one another by an actual physical road.

In the view of the cosmology, the progressive stages of matter could be conceptualized as seven structures or houses (defined by the Egyptian term *arit*) that were separated by gateways or obstacles. Consistent with that outlook, the Maori term *arai* can imply the concept of an "obstacle."[19]

In the Dogon and Egyptian cosmologies, the concept of the emergence of *space* is compared to the opening of a mouth. This process relates to a Dogon word *yala* and correlates to an Egyptian term that is pronounced *auau*. An Egyptian homonym for the word can refer to a dog barking. Although the word is *onomatopoeic* (meaning that the word's pronunciation seems to mimic the sound of a dog's bark), the likely cosmological symbolism is to the < shape made by a dog's mouth as it barks, which calls to mind the image of an expanding dimensional space. From this perspective, it makes sense that the Maori word *auau* also refers to "the bark of a dog."[20]

During the stages of the creation of matter as the Dogon understand them, space loops as it expands to create the seven wrapped bubble-like divisions of the egg-of-the-world. In the Dogon and Egyptian cosmologies, this repetitive looping is compared to the action of a *herald,* a messenger who went from town to town repeating an urgent message. Appropriate to this symbolism, Tregear tells us that the Maori word *auau* can also imply the concept of something that is "frequently repeated." The sound of a dog's bark may also relate to this same aspect of the symbolism in that, in many cases, it is also frequently repeated.

We have previously mentioned that as a way of conceptually categorizing symbols of the tradition, Dogon cosmology defines several four-stage guiding metaphors. Perhaps the most familiar of these is the progression of *water, fire, wind,* and *earth,* which are often cast as four primordial elements of creation. From the perspective of the cosmology, they also seem to align with four conceptual stages of creation. (By this interpretation, *water* represents matter as waves, *fire* represents an act of perception, *wind* represents vibration, and *earth* represents mass or matter.) Given in a more generic form, another comparable progression defines four stages of the construction of a house or building. The first of these stages is defined by the Dogon word *bummo* and the Egyptian word *bu maa,* and it implies the initial concept for a structure. Likely Maori correlates to the term *bu* center on the roots *pu* and *hapu,* which express notions of conception. The second stage is expressed by the Dogon word *yala,* which we see as a likely correlate to the Egyptian and Maori words *ahau* and which relates to the opening up of a defined space. The third stage, during which further definition of the structure is continued, is given by the Dogon word *tonu* and the Egyptian word *tennu*. It seems likely that this relates to the Maori word *tonu,* which Tregear defines to mean "still, continually, right, straight, correct." The last of these four stages relates to the Dogon word *toymu* and the Egyptian word *temau,* both of which mean "complete" and refer to the completion of a fixed, finished structure. It seems likely that these words bear a relationship to the Maori word *tumau,* which means "fixed" or "constant."

In chapter 4, we discussed the Maori word *po* and its likely relationship to the Egyptian words *pau* and *pau-t,* which refer to concepts of mass and matter and of primordial time. On one level, Maori concepts of the po also relate to a shadowy world of darkness or night, and of death, that might also be seen as a correlate to the Egyptian concepts of the Underworld, or Tuat, which was understood as a place that related to death.

12 Yah and Maori Concepts of Creation from Light

In the period following 3000 BCE and in places such as ancient Egypt, one fairly common feature of the ancient traditions we study is the pairing of deities as male/female symbolic counterparts of a single cosmological concept. A good example of this type of pairing is Amen, whom Budge defines as "a serpent-headed god," and his consort Amen-t, whom Budge defines in a following dictionary entry to Amen as "a serpent-headed goddess, counterpart of the preceding."[1] Within the context of the archaic tradition, goddesses predominated, while familiar gods such as Amen, Osiris, and Siva only came into ascendance sometime after 2600 BCE. This circumstance suggests that some male gods may have been later additions to the cosmology, perhaps introduced as part of what we perceive as a broader set of cross-regional revisions and reversals. To the extent that patriarchy came to eventually take precedence, memory of certain mother goddesses may have ultimately been lost within a given culture. If the society saw its beginnings late enough in history, archaic goddesses may have never actually played a role in the culture. This is not to say that masculine elements were not evident within the archaic cosmology, because the surviving philosophies of the earliest traditions indicate that they were.

We have said in a prior book, *Point of Origin,* that the ancient name that the Egyptians assigned to the general region of southeastern Turkey was Getpetkai. Based on the glyph structure of the word and other evidence, we interpreted this to be the archaic name of a mountaintop sanctuary, one that we equate with Gobekli Tepe. We later found that if we applied a more modernized pronunciation to the glyphs of the name, we could alternately read it as Het Pet Ka Yah, a compound of four familiar terms. Symbolic definitions for these terms imply that the name meant "temple (Het) of space (Pet) embracing (Ka) light (Yah)." The name seemed to restate a primary prerequisite for the formation of matter (where the formation of mass goes hand-in-hand with the emergence of space and time): the notion that a masculine material energy associated with the concept of *space* (Pet) comes to be intermingled with a feminine nonmaterial energy characterized as *light* (Yah) to catalyze the structures of our material universe.

However, on a more human level, the suggestion (in keeping with Dogon belief) was that the sanctuary at Gobekli Tepe was also used to facilitate the instruction of material beings (we humans) by capable, knowledgeable nonmaterial beings, with the intention of catalyzing orderly societies within the framework of our material world. This outlook begins with the overt beliefs of ancient cultures such as the Dogon and the Buddhists, who make unequivocal claims that civilizing instruction was passed to humanity at remote locales by beneficent nonhumans. Likewise, there is suggestive evidence in a number of ancient cultures that ties back to the specific era of Gobekli Tepe. Examples of this include Egyptian king lists that give ostensible durations of rule for both historical and quasi-mythical kings. The evidence includes structures such as the Sphinx and the three largest pyramids at Giza, whose proposed alignments may bear a symbolic relationship to the era of 10,000 BCE.

In *Point of Origin* we made the argument that the mountaintop megalithic site of Gobekli Tepe represented an archaic instructional sanctuary, of the type described by the Dogon and the Buddhists, where cosmological knowledge and civilizing skills were taught. We also presented linguistic evidence that seems to associate the site with the name *Yah,* symbolizing "light." Best asserts that there is only one instance in which the actions of the Maori Supreme Being Io (Yah) are discussed within a human context. He cites a Maori myth that tells of how the god Tane "ascended to the realm of Io in order to obtain from him the three baskets or repositories of esoteric knowledge."[2] The Maori reference provides us with possible insights into the meaning of three carved "basket" images that can be seen on a pillar at Gobekli Tepe.

Historical, linguistic, and mythical evidence we see in Polynesia and New Zealand implies that the Maori culture was a later incarnation of the cosmological tradition we have been pursuing and so falls conceptually within the later historic era, rather than the earlier archaic one. We would therefore expect the Maori cosmological tradition to emphasize patriarchal elements rather than matriarchal ones, as it outwardly seems to do. Likewise, linguistic evidence suggests that the Maori have retained a cultural memory of the Neolithic instructional sanctuary on Orkney Island. If true, this would place the origins of the Maori as an independent culture sometime after the era of Skara Brae (circa 3200 BCE). From that perspective, Maori cosmology should also demonstrate the effects of the cross-regional symbolic reversals that we perceive to have taken place in other ancient cultures. However, it is also possible that, through the continuities of ancestry, it reflects traces of the earlier archaic tradition.

Comparisons between Maori cosmology and the symbolism found at Gobekli Tepe begin with the feminine nonmaterial energy, comparable to light, that we interpret to be symbolized by the name *Yah*. The likely Maori correlate to this concept rests with the name *Ao,* which according to Tregear refers to "one of the primal deities who are the unborn Forces of Nature. Ao is the personification of Light and the Upper-world as opposed to Darkness and the Lower-world (po)."[3] Our outlook on the cosmological concept of Yah as it has evolved through discussions in previous volumes of this series is that it properly relates (in Dogon, Hindu, and Egyptian terms) not to the *Upper World* or *Third World* of matter, which is defined as our material world, or to the *Second World* or (as it is represented in some ancient cultures)

Underworld, where matter is reorganized to create the egg-of-the-world. Instead, it relates to the boundary between the *First World,* where matter exists as waves, and the *Second World,* where particles form.

In *The Mystery of Skara Brae,* we cited parallel Hindu and Egyptian Tales of the Seven Houses. In these tales, references that pertain to the name *Yah* are symbolically associated with a sleeping person who wakes up. These mythic references serve to align the concept of Yah with forces that cause matter to essentially awaken or return to consciousness. In other sources, Yah is also tacitly compared to a bird that spreads its wings over "the face of the waters" (comparable to the biblical passage in Genesis) or to the glow of light that spreads out over the ocean just before sunrise and awakens a sleeping person. Such symbolism also exists in the Maori tradition, where according to Best, "The only form of light known at the time the Earth Mother brought forth her offspring was [a] feeble glow emanating from a glow-worm."[4]

From another perspective, Maori cosmology defines seven stages of creation that are all given in relation to phases or aspects of light. These begin with this same dim glimmer from a glowworm, who we are told is named Hine-huruhuru.[5] The Maori term *hine* is a title used only in relation to a girl or young woman,[6] and so this indirectly affirms the view of the Sakti tradition, which associated this initiating light with a feminine principle. The Maori term *huru* refers to "the glow of the sun before rising."[7]

The second Maori phase of light is defined as "the faint light made known by Uepoto when he emerged from the body of the Earth Mother." The Maori term *ue* means "to shake or tremble"[8] and so implies the notion of "vibration." In the mind-set of the ancient cosmology, vibration is one of the first attributes that is assigned to matter after it has been perceived. The word *poto* refers to "a short duration of time."[9] The emergence of the concept of *time* is another attribute that is closely associated within the cosmology with the initial emergence of *mass.*

Best defines the third phase of light as "the form of light that obtained after the separation of the Sky Parent and the Earth Mother. A dim, dusky light." This phase is associated with the Maori term *kakarauri*. The word *raua* refers to the concept of "dualism" (the idea that particles of matter emerge in pairs), which the Dogon define as an underlying principle of creation. *Rauroha* connotes the notion of "spreading" and so implies the emergence of *space*.[10] The term *kaka* refers to "a fiber or a hair," or in the terms of the ancient cosmology and modern string theory, a "thread."[11]

The fourth phase of light is defined as "the form of light known when the heavens were fixed on high, and the Earth Mother turned face down to Rarohenga." The Maori word *raro* means "underside,"[12] and the word *henga* refers to the "hull of a canoe."[13] Taken together, this is the same essential concept of the overturning of matter that underlies the title of the prior book of this series, *The Mystery of Skara Brae*. The image is meant to convey the action of a spinning vortex, comparable to an oceanic whirlpool that would be capable of capsizing a boat.

The fourth stage of creation of matter has special symbolic significance: in the mind-set of the cosmology, the seven stages of matter correlate to processes in the macrocosm that form *seven material universes* (paired with *seven nonmaterial universes* for a total of fourteen). Our four-dimensional universe is designated as the fourth of these. The notion of "the heavens" being "fixed on high" refers to the formation of space, an event that is also symbolized by the concept of the separation of earth and sky.

The fifth phase of light is defined as "a wintry form of light," and it relates to the term *aoao nui*. The term *aoao* is a correlate to the previously discussed term *auau*, which refers to "the opening of space." The Maori term *nui* means "great or large."[14] The concept represented here is that of the continued opening of space.

The sixth phase of light is referred to as "cloudless light," and it is associated with the term *tuarea*. The Maori word *tua* refers to "the far side of a solid body."[15] It also can imply someone who "turns their back to go." The implication is one of rotation, again comparable to the spinning vortex that is associated with the Dogon egg-of-the-world. Also implied is a sense of anticipation of completion and of leaving through a doorway. The word *rea* refers to the "entrance to a basket." When Ogotemmeli wanted to describe the symbolism of the Dogon aligned granary shrine and its conceptual relationship to the egg-of-the-world to Griaule, he illustrated his definitions with an upturned basket.

The seventh and final phase of light is defined as "summer light." In the mind-set of the ancient traditions, the year began in the fall, and so summer might be seen as the final season. This phase is defined by the Maori term *tiahoaho*. Phonetically, it bears a likely relationship to the ancient Chinese term for the egg-of-the-world, which is given as *haohao*. The Maori term *hoahoa* can mean "likeness" or "resemblance" and can be used to refer to a spouse or companion. Alternately, it refers to two women and so may evoke the notion of two Mother Goddesses. From a cosmological perspective, the young woman associated with light that is symbolized by the first stage of matter equates conceptually to the Sakti goddess Dharni Penu, whose name means "luminous" and so could refer to a glow of light. The seventh equates to Tana Penu, the earth mother. The term *mother* carries symbolic associations to a womb, which on one level the completed egg-of-the-world represents. From our perspective, the cosmological term *earth* symbolizes "mass" or "matter." The egg itself, which the Dogon refer to as the po pilu (or in the language of the cosmology, "atom of the elephant"), equates conceptually to Ganesha.

In the symbolism of the archaic tradition (which is in agreement with philosophies that underlie the tradition), the concept of Yah aligns with a *feminine energy*, somewhat akin to a mother who wakes her sleeping child. However, in the Maori tradition, again as in Genesis, Ao has been outwardly recast as a male god. As part of his discussion of the po, Best touches on this same Maori concept of Ao, whom he refers to by the alternate name Io. He writes: "[In] the inner teachings of the old-time lore of the Maori . . . it is shown that the great Io, the Supreme Being, existed prior to matter of any kind, that he dwelt in space ere the earth was formed, and that it was he who caused the earth to come into being."[16]

Best quotes a Maori composition that states:

> *Io dwelt in universal space; the universe was in*
> *darkness; all was water.*
> *Day was not, nor moon, nor light; darkness alone*
> *was; all was water.*[17]

Best goes on to explain (again like the passage in Genesis) that Io next "called upon light to appear, and light dawned across space." Just as light is then separated from darkness in the biblical text, Io causes day to be separated from night in the Maori rendition. Maori dictionary definitions for the word *ao* also preserve this significant creative act, as Tregear tells us that the word *ao* can also refer to "daytime; day as opposed to night" or can mean "to become light."[18]

Depending on the particular phonetics of a given language, we see reflections of this same symbolism of Yah, Ao, or Io in various ancient cultures. In Egypt, we find the meanings expressed by words that are formed from the phonetic root *aa.* On Orkney Island in Northern Scotland, the symbolism plays out in relation to the word *el,* which we explained in *The Mystery of Skara Brae* is also the name of a light god comparable to (and often equated with) Yah. In the Hebrew language, references to Yah can be rendered as two *yud* characters ” (perhaps originally pronounced *yah'd*). In light of the many ongoing comparisons that can be made among Dogon, Egyptian, and Hebrew cosmological words, we interpret these *yuds* as correlates to two *reedleaf glyphs* ⎨⎨ in the Egyptian hieroglyphic language.

There are several different perspectives from which the notion of *reeds* relates symbolically to the light god El or, by association, Yah. By our method of interpreting Egyptian glyphs, a single *reedleaf glyph* implies the notion of "that which is," while two *reedleaf glyphs* placed side by side imply the concept of *existence* (or "that which is, is").

Interestingly, Best cites Maori references relating to Io or Yah that are given with the word *ha,* which he says is sometimes coupled with the name *Io.* Almost as if to echo our interpretation of the Egyptian reedleaf glyphs and Yah, Best asserts that the word *ha* means "to be" or "to exist."[19]

The ocean inlet in Northern Scotland on which the clustered houses of Skara Brae are set is called the Bay of Skaill. We interpret the name *Skaill,* in the context of an ancient naming convention (discussed in prior books of this series) to combine the Egyptian word *skhai* (meaning "to celebrate") and *El,* the name of a light god. Based on arguments presented in *The Mystery of Skara Brae,* we also interpret Orkney Island, where the village of Skara Brae is located, to have been the real-world locale of the Egyptian Field of Reeds. The Greek term for the Field of Reeds was the Elysian Fields. In the Scottish Gaelic language, the term for "island" was *eilean* (a word that also meant "training"), while in the Icelandic language the term was *eyland.* The suggestion is that the name *Elysian* may have combined the name of the god El with a term for "island."

13 Foundational Philosophies in Maori Cosmology

As we have come to understand it, the ancient system of cosmology that we have been pursuing rests on two foundational philosophies. The first of these, broadly familiar to modern audiences, is the philosophy of *yoga*. It centers on concepts of personal enlightenment that are rooted in the human body, meditation, physicality, fertility, and the personal psyche. Adherents of this philosophy in the archaic Sakti Cult were a group of enlightened women called Yoginis. The Yoginis fostered an esoteric tradition that was passed down from generation to generation by oral tradition, in very much the same way that Dogon cosmology is structured and transmitted. A class of Dogon priests called the Hogon (a term that is phonetically similar to *Yogini*) are likely modern-day counterparts to these women. The second archaic philosophy on which the cosmology rests is a lesser-known yogic tradition called Samkhya Darshan, which represents a fully realized outlook on the processes by which reality is said to be created. The Sanskrit word *samkhya* is a compound of the terms *sam,* meaning "correct," "proper," or "discriminative," and *khya,* meaning "knowing." Our primary source for information about this philosophy is a book called *Samkhya Darshan: Yogic Perspectives on Theories of Realism* by Swami Niranjanananda Saraswati.

A likely Dogon correlate to the term *Samkhya* combines the Dogon word *sa,* which means "clear,"[1] the word *am,* which implies "knowledge," and the word *kaya,* meaning "expression" or "spoken conceptual word."[2] Combined, these definitions seem sensible, since within the Dogon culture, cosmological knowledge is commonly characterized as "the clear word." In ancient Egypt, the term *sa* referred to the concept of "wisdom or knowledge deified."[3] Budge defines the Egyptian term *Kha* as the name of a god or group of gods whose role he does not actually define. However, the name is written with a glyph 𓎗 that arguably depicts the formation of mass or matter symbolically.[4] In part because the *s* phoneme is not vocalized in their language, the Maori have no direct phonetic correlate to the term *Samkhya.* There are perspectives from which the term can be paired with the Maori word *mahea,* meaning "clear" or "free from obstruction."[5] A related word *maheahea* means "to perceive indistinctly." In any case, many of the fundamental tenets of the Samkhya Darshan philosophy are clearly attested in the Maori culture. The presence of these in conjunction with many of the key terms, symbols, and practices of the cosmological tradition suggests that we can infer the likely influence of a similar underlying philosophy.

Our entry point to these Maori philosophies comes from a 1983 book on the symbolic structure of the Maori culture called *Counterpoint in Maori Culture,* written by anthropologists F. Allan Hanson and Louise Hanson. Their working thesis is that the structures of traditional Maori institutions rest on two dynamic structural forms, defined as *complementarity* and *symmetry.*[6] From the perspective of the ancient cosmology, these can be seen as conceptual equivalents to two foundational principles of Dogon cosmology, defined as *duality* and *parallelism* (symmetry) and the notion of the *pairing of opposites* (complementarity).

Within the context of the thesis of the Hansons, these principles of the Maori tradition evolve from a premise that was promoted by anthropologist and ethnologist Claude Lévi-Strauss called *bricolage.* This term represents the notion that a culture's mode of thinking is shaped by objects and relationships found in their everyday experience. This outlook is a reversed match for the perspective of Dogon society, where it is understood that cosmological thought was intentionally defined in relation to everyday experiences so as to imbue the acts of daily life with mnemonic value, to reinforce the teachings of an instructed cosmology.

While within the philosophy of Samkhya Darshan creation arises as the consequence of the introduction of male and female energies, the Hansons write of the Maori and bricolage that "particularly important in the modeling of reality on this basis was the bifurcation of humanity into sexes." The Hansons quote Best as stating that for the Maori, "Everything has its male and female element."[7] This symbolism extended even as far as to the bilateral symmetry of the human body, where the right side was considered to be male and the left side female. Comparable symbolism is implied in other ancient cultures such as the Dogon, whose practice it was to bury a male body lying on its right side and a female body on its left.

Similar concepts of sexuality and fertility are understood to have been central to the philosophies of the archaic matriarchal tradition from which we believe many of the later classic traditions emerged. In keeping with that outlook, the cosmological processes of creation are conceptualized as beginning with an *embrace* between a *female energy* and a *male energy*. This concept of an embrace is what we infer to be symbolized by the pair of carved arms and hands that wrap around the end of a pillar at the Gobekli Tepe megalithic site. Similarly, the Hansons write that for the Maori, "in the beginning the earth and sky were locked together in a lovers' embrace."[8]

As a real-world parallel, concepts of gender and sexual opposites make natural correlates to astrophysical processes that rest on notions of duality and the pairing of opposites. It is for this reason that, in ancient cosmology, the few stages of cosmological creation that cannot be thought of as having a dual nature (such as the single act of perception that is said to catalyze the formation of matter) are often expressed symbolically in relation to a *masturbatory* or *incestuous* act, a sexual/creative act that falls outside the expected partnered-pair paradigm.

Along these same lines, the Dogon see direct parallels as existing between the processes of biological reproduction and those of the formation of matter and of the universe. From this perspective the pairing of opposing forces, conceived of as opposite sexes, underlies the symbolism of creation for many cultures. The Hansons define a similar principle at work in the Maori culture, where they say the Maori "used the complementary structure of sexual union followed by the production of offspring to conceptualize the origin of [diverse] things."[9] The principle is most overtly expressed in a quote that opens the second chapter of *Counterpoint in Maori Culture,* which the Hansons attribute to Nepia Pokuhu, a Maori priest from New Zealand who lived in the mid-1800s. The quote reads, "To be clear on this: all things issue forth from Rangi and Papa; nothing which can be imagined came from Papa alone, or from Rangi alone."[10]

On the macroscopic level of the formation of the universe, the Dogon priests describe the configuration of elements that preceded an event comparable to the *big bang* as involving two *inward-facing thorns* (perhaps structures comparable to two *black holes*) that fed matter inward and confined it gravitationally as if inside an *egg*. As this constrained matter spun more and more quickly, it eventually reached a state where the gravity of the black holes that introduced the matter was no longer strong enough to contain it. The egg ruptured and scattered matter to all corners of the universe, in the words of the Dogon "like pellets of clay." Maori mythology includes an episode whose proper symbolic interpretation may be similar to that of this Dogon storyline. In the Maori myth, two large hills (one described as male, the other female) fell in love. Their embrace blocked the flow of a river, whose waters then backed up to form a lake. In the Maori rendition of the tale, a magician recognizes the situation as being an improper one and uses his magic to restore the flow of the river.[11]

From the perspective of the philosophy of Samkhya Darshan, it is the interaction between the *nonmaterial* and *material universes* that facilitates life in the material realm. This interaction is characterized by an inward and outward flow of *energy*. In the human sphere of the Maori culture, the Hansons characterize that godly influences were understood to result from the "union in the complementary relationship between physical and spiritual beings."[12] The Hansons are careful to assert this perspective as a kind of tool of analysis, rather than make any literal claim for the earthly presence of spiritual beings. However, the viewpoint resonates with overt claims made on the part of cultures such as the Dogon and Buddhists for actual, emanated spiritual energy.

However, the view of the archaic Sakti Cult was that attempts to communicate *knowledge* were also routinely made between the nonmaterial and material domains. This communication could take the form of vivid images or events that might appear in dreams, auspicious astronomic signs, or unusual movements or behaviors of animals. Communication from a nonmaterial realm was also understood to occur through what we might perceive as unlikely coincidences. The Hansons tell us that concepts parallel to these existed in the Maori culture, conceptualized as the communication of the *atua* (the notion of *the infinite* that is interpreted by some as *gods*) with the human world.[13] These atua are described in terms that would be comparable to fairies in Scotland and Ireland, and the Hansons actually refer to them as fairies. They write, "In certain respects [these] fairies were ethereal beings . . . yet fairies were corporeal enough."[14] The atua interacted directly with humans, took the form of animals, and could be the source of "apparently random events." They were also understood to be the source of omens. In the words of Augustus Earle, a New Zealand resident who observed and wrote about the Maori, "There is not a wind that blows but they imagine it bears some message from [the atua]."[15] The Hansons state that messages from the atua needed to be interpreted symbolically and that a class of skilled experts called *tohungas* ("skilled persons") was required to interpret them. Appropriate to this outlook, Tregear informs us that Maori words for "omen" included the terms *aitua* and *tohu*.[16]

In the definitions of the philosophy of Samkhya Darshan, the truthful knowledge that can be attained by an individual in the evoked multiplicity of the material realm is referred to as *mahat*.[17] The Maori term *maha* means "many."[18] In ancient Egypt the likely correlate is the familiar term *maat,* which is treated in the context of "correct knowledge." The Maori term *ma* means "white," "pale," and "clean," terms and concepts that we associate with the instructed knowledge of the cosmology and with the nonmaterial universe.

Within Samkhya Darshan, the ascent or manifestation of the elements is defined by the term *ahamkara.* A likely Maori correlate to this word is *marama,* meaning "to rise up."[19] The same term forms the root of a Maori word for "enlightenment."

From the perspective of the Samkhya Darshan philosophy, humanity is confined within ascending cycles of growth and enlightenment that compare with the Hindu cycles of *karmic rebirth.* The *confinement* or *bondage* comes out of a kind of false identification, in which an individual is understandably convinced that the illusion of everyday experience represents true reality.[20] Liberation from this cycle is arrived at through the attainment of a kind of discriminating knowledge, defined as *enlightenment,* that ultimately allows a person to distinguish between *existence* and *nonexistence.* Consistent with that outlook, the Maori concept of *knowledge* can be expressed by the words *uhumanea*[21] and *ihumanea.*[22] The term *uhumanea* combines the phonetic root *uhu,* meaning "cramped" (a synonym for the concept of "confined"), and what is arguably the term *human.* A similar linguistic relationship between the notions of *confinement* and *knowledge* is expressed by the Egyptian word *khent,* which means "confined" but also is the term for a "shrine, sanctuary, or temple," locales that were intimately associated with instructed knowledge.[23] In ancient Egypt, each temple included a *House of Life* and a *House of Books,* places where civilizing skills were preserved and taught.

14 Maori References to the Field of Arou

In the prior volume of this series, *The Mystery of Skara Brae,* we discussed a series of megalithic sites on Orkney Island in Northern Scotland that date from the Neolithic period, around 3200 BCE. In our view, these sites were meant to illustrate, on a human scale, the progressive stages of the formation of matter. We know the sites were interrelated because they were linked to one another in Neolithic times by a road, which due to the placement of the sites traced the shape of a large counterclockwise spiral around intervening bodies of water. The spiral calls to mind a Dogon figure that, on one level of interpretation, characterizes their egg-of-the-world. We have said that from one perspective, the egg is compared to seven rays of a star of increasing length, and the spiral is drawn to inscribe the endpoints of those rays.

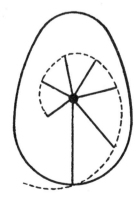

The spiral within the Dogon
egg-of-the-world (from
Forde, *African Worlds,* 84)

The Orkney Island road, which was set beside a body of water called Stenness, began at a standing stone called the Watchstone of Stenness, then led to a megalithic stone circle known as the Standing Stones of Stenness. The road continued on to a once peaked (now domed) burial chamber called Maes Howe and then ultimately onward to a cluster of eight stone chambers or houses that constituted the tiny farming village of Skara Brae. The progression of figures that are enshrined in stone on the island coincides with the sequence of geometric shapes that underlie matter and that, for the Dogon, generate the clustered dimensions of the egg-of-the-world.

However, the full Dogon concept of this progression includes developmental stages for matter that go several steps beyond the chambered egg. In the mind-set of Dogon cosmology, the next conceptual stage relates to vibrational frequencies that define fundamental particles of matter and that differentiate them from what modern astrophysicists refer to as "the background field." Each year at the time of the planting of seeds for a new agricultural season, the Dogon illustrate this concept symbolically by drawing the figure of a circle in the middle of the agricultural field of their highest-ranking priest, known as the Arou Priest. Next, they fill the circle with a series of zigzag lines that symbolize the vibrational frequencies of these particles. Because the field belongs to the Arou Priest we refer to it as the Field of Arou. This Dogon practice suggests that the Orkney Island symbolism might have actually extended beyond the cluster of eight houses at Skara Brae and on to the agricultural field that is understood to have adjoined them.

On one conceptual level, it is clear that the Field of Arou represented a cosmological concept and was meant to be understood symbolically. However, on a second level of understanding, it also constituted an actual physical field that the Dogon planted with seeds and cultivated to grow food. In *The Mystery of Skara Brae,* we were exploring possible ancient Egyptian influences on Orkney Island, and so it made sense to look for possible Egyptian correlates to this Dogon concept. One Egyptian word for "field" was given as *sekhet* or *skhet,* and dictionary searches based on that word turned up a comparable Egyptian concept called the Sekhet Aaru. Budge, in his *Egyptian Hieroglyphic Dictionary,* interprets the term *Sekhet Aaru* to mean "Field of Reeds," a term that defines the Egyptian concept of an afterlife. This was also the concept on which the later Greek notion of the Elysian Fields was based.

Like the Dogon Field of Arou, both Greek and Egyptian sources treat the concepts of the Field of Reeds and Elysian Fields on two conceptual levels—as a mythical concept, but also as an actual physical locale. Ancient texts that provide details of the physical locale describe it in terms that also correctly describe Orkney Island. It is portrayed as an idyllic white island located along the edge of the Western ocean, a place of great winds surrounded by ocean inlets and intimately associated with an agricultural field. The language used in some of the texts also evokes Orkney Island. The locale is actually referred to by the Greek poet Pindar as Okeanos. The term *Elysian* could well be formed from a root word that means "island." Ancient Scandinavian names for Orkney Island were Argat and Orkneyar. Based on Dogon and Egyptian references, we associate the island with the terms *arou* or *aaru* and with the phoneme *ar.*

The effort required to conceive of, design, and raise the series of megalithic structures on Orkney Island suggests that it must have been a significant center of culture, civilizing skills, and knowledge in Neolithic times. Perhaps reflective of that view, a Maori word *aroa* that means "to understand" takes a phonetic form that is quite similar to *arou.*[1] Likewise, there are attributes of the site and its known history (which we cite in *The Mystery of Skara Brae*) that link it conceptually with Dogon and Buddhist notions of ancient civilizing instruction. The accepted archaeological dating of the Skara Brae site at around 3200 BCE is, developmentally speaking, too early to reasonably reflect distant influences of dynastic Egypt, and yet many of the symbolic aspects of Orkney Island fall directly in line with Dogon and Egyptian cultural elements we have been exploring. An alternative viewpoint, based on Dogon and Buddhist claims of instructed knowledge, is that Orkney Island may have constituted a campus-like instructional sanctuary whose educational benefits ultimately flowed in the reverse direction: from Orkney Island toward the agriculturally based monarchies that are known to have arisen in various regions of the world during the period just following 3200 BCE. From that perspective, Egyptian ancient concepts of heaven (in the form of the Field of Reeds and its companion, the Field of Offerings) can be seen to align with those of any successful college student who may have been truly fond of his or her educational experience and so might have difficulty imagining a better environment to return to after death than the one that had been enjoyed during the years of study.

Attributes of the nearby Faroe Islands, which are situated a short distance to the north and west of the Orkney Islands, suggest that they might have served as a kind of safe haven for the theoretic instructors of this Neolithic tradition. In support of that view, the ancient Egyptian word for "pharaoh" (*per-aa*) originally referred to a place, not the person who lived there. Meanwhile, the Faroe Islands themselves offer a number of different natural defenses against unwanted visitors and so in our view would make an excellent home base for any knowledgeable group who might have organized this ancient instructional effort. Likewise, there is no currently accepted academic theory for the origins of the Egyptian pharaohs. No one knows with certainty where they came from, which cultural tradition they represented, or precisely how they came to power sometime after 3100 BCE in Egypt. The earliest kings from widespread regions of the world claimed a right to power that was ostensibly delegated to them from "gods." Such statements could make sense if one purpose of the Orkney Island site was to train leaders for regional monarchy and for the priesthood.

Another Dogon cosmological term that is applied to the spiral of matter associated with the egg-of-the-world and to aligned shrines comparable to a Buddhist stupa is *arq* or *ark*. In *The Mystery of Skara Brae,* we associated this phonetic root with an archaic name for Orkney Island, which was Argat. Similar phonetics can be seen in the name of an Egyptian sanctuary: *arq-hehtt*. The phonetics of these words helps us put in perspective a Maori title for priests previously mentioned, which Tregear gives as *ariki*. However, the Maori word also carries a second meaning that has mythic significance for ancient Egypt, most obviously in regard to the biblical story of the Exodus from Egypt, which is "firstborn." The term "firstborn" was also a title of the high priest of Ptah. Linguistics provides us with a similar possible linkage to the much earlier era of Gobekli Tepe by way of an Egyptian word *tepi* that also means "firstborn."

We associate the term *Sekhet Aaru* with Orkney Island, but also most specifically with the agricultural field that would have adjoined Skara Brae. In ancient Egypt, the Field of Reeds was described as having been positioned nearby what is called the Field of Offerings, or Sekhet Hetep. From a cosmological perspective, the concept of an *offering* as a thing "given" arguably relates to the notion of a *dimension,* a concept that is treated as a given in creational science. Geometric figures such as a *point,* a *line,* a *space,* and *mass* that we associate with the Orkney Island megalithic structures also bear a relationship to the concept of *dimensions* of matter.

The Egyptian word *skhet* can refer to the spiral shape that defines the progressive stages of matter. We noted in *China's Cosmological Prehistory* that the ancient Chinese term for this same structure is given as *haohao.* For the Maori, the concept of a "religious offering" is expressed by the similar word *hau.* Tregear states as a prelude to his dictionary entry for the word *hau:* "This word is an exceedingly difficult one to arrange or classify under different headings. Many of its meanings seem sharply distinct from the others; but those who read the comparatives carefully will see that it is almost impossible to tell where one meaning merges into another, or where a dividing line could be drawn. Thus the sense of cool, fresh, wind, dew, eager, brisk, famous, illustrious, royal, commanding, giving orders, striking, hewing, etc. all pass into one another. Therefore, with regret, I have to group all of the meanings of *hau* together."[2]

Clustered meanings are one of the signature features of terms of the cosmology. Maori meanings for the word *hau* touch on a variety of aspects of climate, instructed agriculture, and the fostering of kingships that we associate with Orkney Island.

We have mentioned that the archaic tradition that we believe descended from Gobekli Tepe was a matriarchal one, characterized primarily by Mother Goddesses. Within a few centuries of the beginning of the dynastic era in Egypt, reversals in cosmological symbolism occurred that resulted in the predominance of Creator Gods over Mother Goddesses. From this perspective, the Maori religion, which is largely characterized by gods such as Tane and mythic cultural heroes like Maui, who was thrown into the sea as an infant and saved by the ocean spirits, reflects a cosmological mind-set that is consistent with the historical era following 2600 BCE, rather than the earlier archaic tradition. So it seems reasonable to think that the Maori may have been among the cultures who were influenced by Orkney Island instruction. If so, then we might expect to find surviving cultural references to the era of Orkney Island instruction among the Maori. And, in fact, it seems that we do.

Words that arguably bear a phonetic relationship to the Dogon and Egyptian words *arou* and *aaru* define key cosmological concepts within the Maori tradition. The first of these, pronounced *ahurewa,* refers to "a sacred place."[3] In his dictionary entry for the term, Tregear refers the reader to the phonetic roots of the word: *ahu* and *rewa.* Comparable to the Dogon and Egyptian phonetic root *ar,* which implies the concept of ascension and is symbolized by the notion of a high hill or a staircase, the Maori term *ahu* means "to heap up" or "to foster." The Maori word *rewa* means "sacred." Together the words express a concept that may be an effective equivalent of the *ascending stages of creation* that we associate with the term *arou,* the idea of the *upward fostering of the sacred.* We have mentioned previously that the term *ara* means "to rise up" or "to awake," definitions that relate directly to the cosmological concept of the ascension of matter.[4] The idea that the Orkney Island complex of

Arou might have played an instructional role in ancient times may also be reflected in a Maori term *aroa*, which means "to understand."

In *The Mystery of Skara Brae,* one of the first positive links we were able to make between the structures on Orkney Island and the Dogon creation tradition rested with the form of the Neolithic houses that are found at Skara Brae. The plan and construction method of the earliest of the Skara Brae houses, characterized by local Scottish researchers as including "unique" features, is an outward match for a traditional Dogon stone house. As the Dogon understand the architectural form, it is meant to replicate the body of a woman who is sleeping. The structure includes a round room at one end that symbolizes a head, two rectangular sleeping areas on the side that represent arms, a central room with a hearth that represents the body cavity and heart, and a doorway at the other end that represents the woman's sexual parts. The idea that a Dogon house would relate symbolically to their system of cosmology seems particularly sensible, since one of the generic metaphors by which symbols can be classified within the Dogon system is correlated to four stages in the construction of a house. So it seems significant that a Maori term that means "to build or erect a house," *ahuahu,* bears a close phonetic resemblance to the term *Arou,* or *Aaru,* an ancient name we apply to the place where we believe this symbolism originated.

Tregear explains that another Maori name for the region of Ahurewa is Naherangi, meaning "blow softly as the gentle breeze; place where the wind comes from." Windiness is one of the characteristic aspects of the climate at Orkney Island, and it is also cited in ancient Egyptian and Greek texts as a signature attribute of the Field of Reeds and of the Elysian Fields.

When the agriculturally based kingship of the First Dynasty took hold at Abydos in Egypt sometime after 3100 BCE, it made its appearance in association with a temple-based academy called the House of Life. If we endorse an interpretation of Orkney Island as a kind of instructional sanctuary, then it is possible that the Egyptian concept of the House of Life was intended to provide continued instruction to priestly initiates of the cosmological tradition, comparable to what appears to have been offered on Orkney Island. The Maori culture established a similar temple-based school of instruction at the temple of Wharekura. In his dictionary entry for the term, Tregear states that it was "a kind of college or school in which anciently the sons of priest-chiefs (*ariki*) were taught mythology, history, agriculture, astronomy, etc."[5]

Dogon concepts relating to their field of the Arou Priest have meanings on both physical and mythic/cosmological levels of understanding. The same is true for how Egyptian sources treat the concept of the Sekhet Aaru, or the Field of Reeds, and how Greek writers presented their concept of the Elysian Fields. Some references fall in the realm of cosmology, while others seem to be given in relation to specific real-world geography. So we would expect the same could be true for any related Maori references. Both in his dictionary and in other works, Tregear discusses the mythic-versus-real duality that surrounds the fabled Maori homeland of Hawaiki, and more particularly in regard to the great temple of Wharekura that was said to have been located there. He also felt that the consistent use of the same term, *wharekura,* in relation both to the actual temple and to schools in New Zealand added to the confusion.[6]

In his book *The Maori Race,* Tregear comments that, in the Cook Islands, concepts of this Maori homeland seem closely associated with the Spirit World. He also remarks about the close real-world proximity in which the Upper World and Lower World seem to take their placement in some Maori myths. For example, in one myth a character is able to view the cliffs of the Upper World from the Lower World; in another, the great winds of the Lower World lie just below the feet of characters of the Upper World, who can look down and see "fire, men, trees and ocean," as well as people going about their real-world pursuits. Several of the Faroe Islands are characterized by vertical cliffs that rise hundreds of feet upward from the surrounding ocean passages. Almost daily, whirlwind-like storms make their way through these passages, but with effects that are almost unnoticeable from the clifftops of the islands. People who stand atop one of these islands can quite literally look down on activities occurring below them. Once again, both the geographic and meteorologic attributes described in the Maori myths match characteristics of the Faroe and Orkney Islands in Northern Scotland.

The Maori term *mu* refers to "an ancestor of the Maori," while the Maori term *mua* refers to "the front" or "forepart" of something.[7] These meanings align well with the Egyptian word *mu,* which referred both to a person's female relatives and to the concept of an *ancestress.* Also, as with many ancient cultures, the Dogon conceptualize the era of the past as being "ahead" of us, rather than "behind" us, as we think of it in the modern view. An example to illustrate how the concept was perceived is that of a bus filled with a person's genetic ancestors, where the oldest (those who metaphorically "get off the bus" first) are seated at the front. From that perspective, the "future" conceptually follows (or is behind) the "the past." Tregear defines the related term *mua* as "a god worshipped in the temple of Wharekura."

Supportive of the outlook of a possible relationship between the temple of Wharekura of the Maori and the Egyptian temple-based concept of the House of Life, the Maori term *whare* means "house" or "hut"[8] and the word *kura* refers to the "color red."[9] However, *kura* also refers to a kind of *red grass* used to form wreaths that were worn by the mythical Maori Chiefs of the Migration, those who ostensibly led the Maori to New Zealand. A myth tells of how, after one of these wreaths was thrown into the water, the red grass it was woven with took root and spread. That grass is said to still be found growing near the city of Auckland. The strong implication is that the word *kura* refers to "red reeds" of the variety from New Zealand. From that perspective, the Maori term *Wharekura* could be interpreted to mean "House of Reeds." If that interpretation is a correct one, then the symbolism could well be to the inferred school at the Field of Reeds on Orkney Island, whose cosmology inheres in the architectural form of a house and which was seemingly replicated at the Maori temple.

The earliest Scandinavian visitors to Orkney Island reported encountering two groups of residents living there. The first were described as pygmies of strange habits called the Peti, and the second were a group of clerics called the Papae, who were said to always wear white. In *The Mystery of Skara Brae,* we presented evidence to link the Peti with a group of mythical teachers of the Dogon called the Nummo, who were credited with having instructed the Dogon in skills such as agriculture. Some references that may pertain to the Peti describe them as a group of sorcerers, while others seem to link them to the ancient Scottish descriptions of fairies. We associate the Papae with the Dogon themselves, who are commonly characterized as a priestly tribe. Dogon sources describe the Nummo as having a need to always be nearby bodies of water. In Maori mythology, the name *Petipeti* referred to a "marine deity" who was considered to have been an ancestor to the Maori priests.[10] The Maori term *papa* can mean "father," a term that was traditionally applied to clerics and priests in Scotland. The word is based on the phonetic root *pa,* which refers to a mythical "god who presided over consuming food."[11]

15 The Wharekura, or School of Reeds

Along with a wealth of other information found in his 1904 book *The Maori Race,* Tregear provides us with many informative details about the functioning of the Wharekura schools in the Maori culture. Tregear tells us that, in addition to the Wharekura school for training priests mentioned earlier, similar schools came to be associated with each Maori tribe, very much as a House of Life and House of Books, also described as priestly schools, were associated with each Egyptian temple in ancient times. Descriptions of how these schools were conceptually organized, along with details of the practical functioning of the schools, are given in chapter 17 of Tregear's book. He writes, "Ancient legends seem to establish the fact that in some far off country there was a great temple called Whare-kura, the 'Holy House.' The locality is said to have been known as Uawa."[1]

According to Best, other names besides Wharekura (or Wharekura) were also applied to the schools. These are given as Whaire Maire, Whaire Takiura, Whare Puri, Whare Wananga, and Whare Purakau. The Maori word *maire* refers to "a tree having very hard wood,"[2] perhaps comparable to an oak tree. The word *takiura* refers to "sacred food cooked at ceremonies."[3] In his book *Tuhoe, the Children of the Mist* (presented as an overview of pre-Maori cultures in New Zealand), Best writes, "The word *wananga* seems to be applied to occult knowledge, and *purakau* to traditions and myths, but the meaning of *puri* is not so clear to the writer. Possibly some obliging ethnographer will trace it back to the great temple of Jagah-nath at Puri, in Orissa, where tree worship and barber priests obtained."[4]

Of course, Orissa is the modern name of the region of India that is the seat of worship for the archaic Sakti Cult, from which we trace the early roots of the cosmology of our studies. Jagah-nath is a nondenominational (or cross-denominational) surrogate of the Hindu god Vishnu and has associations with a number of different traditions in India, specifically including the Sakti Cult. Those connections would seemingly make our role in these passages that of the rhetorical ethnographer of Best's offhand suggestion.

In Best's view, the variant names applied to the schools reflected differences in the subject matter taught. From that perspective, myths and traditions would have been taught at the Whare Purakau schools, while occult knowledge would have been emphasized at the Whare Wananga schools. Such division of instruction goes hand in hand with a precept of the Maori culture that precluded a student of cosmology from also pursuing occult knowledge. Based on Dogon phonetics, students at the Whare Puri schools would likely have studied cosmology and agriculture, since their term *puru* relates to the concept of "disorder in the dispersion of spiritual forces."[5] *Disorder* is the domain of the Dogon Second World of matter, where matter, originally found in a perfect wavelike state, comes to be reordered. The stages of this Second World are what are reflected in the megalithic symbolism on Orkney Island, given in relation to the cultivated Field of Arou. In support of this viewpoint, a second Dogon word *puru* refers to "cultivated grains."

Franceso Brighenti, the author of a book called *Sakti Cult of Orissa*, makes frequent reference to the temple in India at Puri as one of a handful of sites with legitimate claims of association with the most archaic eras of the tradition.[6] However, he also expresses confusion that the Mother Goddess who was celebrated there was associated with one of the destructive aspects of the Sakta tradition. The Dogon sense of the term *puru*, which is rooted in the concept of the disruption of matter in its wavelike state and the subsequent reordering of matter as particles, provides a sensible rationale for the seemingly counterintuitive symbolism at Puri.

Tregear writes that the term *Wharekura* was "transferred on the arrival of the Maori in New Zealand to tribal buildings with something of the old attributes."[7] Because the name given to these schools, *Wharekura,* is a match for that of a mythical sacred place of ancient instruction located far to the east, any clear definition of the term must properly begin with what is still known about that ancient school. The meaning of School of Reeds that we interpret for the Maori term, its phonetic similarity to the word *arou,* or *aaru,* and the stated locale and purposes of the ancient school all lead us to associate the Maori tradition with that of Orkney Island, as discussed in *The Mystery of Skara Brae.* From this perspective, the name of Tregear's mythical locality, *Uawa,* would correspond to the name *Arou* or *Aaru* that we assign to the agricultural field on Orkney Island. The compound term *Whare-kura* would likely combine that same name and a Faroese word for "house of worship," given as *kirkja.* Together the terms *Arou Kirkja* would refer to the Neolithic sanctuary located on Orkney Island, or the "house of worship located at Arou."

Tregear describes the surviving Maori accounts of the ancient Wharekura school as being "fragmentary and shadowy,"[8] yet among the Maori, a very specific understanding has been preserved of the physical shape of the structure in which the original school was housed. Tregear includes a diagram of a horseshoe-shaped enclosure, comparable to an ancient stone structure called a *fulacht fiadh* (plural: *fulachta fiadh*) that is commonly found in Ireland. Similar structures have also been excavated on Orkney Island.

One researcher of these sites, an archaeologist from Belfast, Ireland, named Anne-Marie Nurnberger (née Denvir) writes of the Irish structures, "Fulachta fiadh were an integral part of the prehistoric landscape in Ireland, they provide significant evidence of activity in areas with little artifact deposition. They also form the biggest number of a single

Fulacht fiadh cooking pit (photo by David Hawgood)

prehistoric monument in Ireland and over the years have generated much interest in the archaeological world. Yet the purpose of fulachta fiadh is still unclear even though many major studies have been undertaken on them."[9]

Similarly, a website for the Society of Antiquaries of Scotland states, "There are currently over 1900 burnt mound sites recorded in Scotland, with the highest concentrations occurring in Shetland, Orkney, Caithness and Sutherland, and in Southern Scotland around Dumfries and Galloway. It has been suggested that this distribution is representative of the original spread of hot stone technologies."[10]

Like many of the place names and designations given by early cultures in Scotland and Ireland, the term *fulacht* (or *fulachta*) *fiadh* is of uncertain origin and meaning. In an article from the *Journal of Irish Archaeology*, John Ó Néill writes, "Many commentators suggest that the Irish word *'fulacht'* denotes a pit used for cooking. *'Fiadh'* in Old Irish meant something like 'wild,' often relating to animals such as deer. However, all commentators acknowledge significant difficulties in deriving a genuine etymology for the word *'fulacht.'* As some historical references clearly use the term *'fulacht'* to describe a cooking spit, a close reading of these accounts suggests that the term actually derives from a word meaning 'support' and probably carries a deliberate reference to the Irish words for blood and meat."[11]

However, another potentially viable perspective on the word *fiadh* is that it derives from the same root as the word *Filidha,* a Druidic term that refers to a learned class of seers and teachers. Miranda J. Green of the University of Wales writes in her book *The World of the Druids:*

> Many Graeco-Roman writers give the Druids a thoroughly bad press. . . . Other writers present [them as] profound thinkers, intellectuals, and philosophers, scholars of the universe, teachers, and custodians of oral culture. . . . Despite the inherent difficulties of constructing an accurate and complete timeline, [evidence attests to] the longevity of Druidism, even though its character underwent radical changes between its first mention in Gaul and Britain, at the end of the first millennium BC, and the Neo-Pagan Druidry currently practiced in Britain, Europe and the rest of the world. Druidism, then, has existed in some guise for over two millennia.[12]

The commonly shared horseshoe shape of the Maori and Irish structures suggests a conceivable connection between the word *fiadh* and the Maori word *pihao,* which means "to enclose, as to encompass a fish."[13] In the Dogon culture, initiates undergoing such training were referred to as *fish.* Similarly, as implied by Tregear, the Maori term *whare* can mean "house."[14] A *wharau* is a "hut or shed made of branches," the same definition that applies to the Egyptian word *skhet,* a term that we argue defines the instructional sanctuary on Orkney Island.[15] If we allow the possibility of a correlation for these structures to the Maori, then one conceivable purpose of the structure was as a school for the instruction of initiates in the civilizing concepts associated with cosmology. If, as for the Maori, each tribe or village established its own school, that could account for the great number of structures reported by archaeologists. Moreover, when we explore possible phonetic roots for the word *fiadh* in the enigmatic Faroese language, found in the region of Orkney Island, we discover that the word *felag* means "academy."[16] The Faroese word *folkaatk* implies the meaning "of the folk" or "of the people." Looked at from this perspective, the two terms *folkaatk felag* in combination (comparable to *fulachta fiadh*) could imply the meaning of "people's academy."

Other linguistic similarities can be cited to suggest potential links between the Maori schools and the Dogon and ancient Egyptian cultures. For example, according to Tregear, the chief priest of the Wharekura temple held the title of *paroro,* a word that bears a phonetic resemblance to both the Dogon term for chieftainship, *faro,* and the Egyptian title *pharaoh.*[17]

Tregear informs us in *The Maori Race* that, like shrines we have studied in the Buddhist and Dogon traditions that were aligned along an east-west axis, the structure of the Wharekura was "carefully oriented, its front being eastward."[18] Similarly, the name was also understood to define a circular enclosure at whose symbolic center rested the notion of a creator god, a deity named Kahukura, who was known as the *rainbow god.* In *Point of Origin,* we discussed similar symbolic associations between the circular base of a shrine and colors of light, along with a center point that was deemed to represent all of the colors combined.

Typically, the Maori schools were devoted to classes of instruction. In the first, which pertained only to the ariki candidates for priesthood, instruction was given in mythology, astronomy, history, and the "mysteries of life and death." Students who were not on the track toward the priesthood were taught skills of agriculture and "practical astronomy," a term that referred to astronomic skills that related to the agricultural calendar, which were required for the planting and harvesting of crops.[19] Instruction for boys generally began when they were twelve years old and lasted for three to five years. Although as a general rule no woman was allowed in the school building, the opening ceremony was attended by an elder priestess. This detail might possibly constitute a remnant of the archaic matriarchal tradition, from which we trace the later cosmologies.

Classes were conducted over the course of four or five months per year, running from autumn until springtime. Instruction began with a priest who, prior to the commencement of any religious instruction, recounted the history of the tribe. By tradition, each of the instructor-priests spoke in turn, and only one spoke at a time. The first month of instruction was devoted to the subject of the primary gods of the Maori tradition. Once completed, it was followed by tutelage in incantations and witchcraft. Certain of the most sacred incantations were not allowed to be recited indoors but were explicitly reserved for use in the woods and mountains. According to Tregear, instruction ended at midnight each night, and the students slept during the daytime. Students were not allowed to go to places where food was being cooked, but instead food was brought to, or provided by, the school.

During the months of recess, the students' resolve to maintain secrecy regarding the details of their instruction was routinely tested, with their friends encouraged to try to coax information from them. Those who were found, against prohibitions, to have revealed privileged information were expelled from the school. Meals were taken in the building, but sleeping there was prohibited. Because laws of tapu applied to the students during their months of instruction, and thereby transferred a kind of sacred quality to them, they were not allowed to associate with tribe members who were deemed to be nonsacred.

At the completion of a student's course of instruction, a final incantation called the *whaka-pou* was recited, whose purpose was to firmly establish the teachings of the priests in the mind of the student. Tregear relates that the Maori word *poua* means "fixed." The student was then taken to an altar (consisting of an upright stone or a shrine) and instructed to hurl a flat rock or stone. If the stone broke, it was taken as a sign that the student had not properly assimilated the teachings. If the stone remained whole, a second test was applied and an incantation called *hoa* was recited, whose purpose was, by willpower only, to make the stone vibrate. The incantation was conceptualized as a vehicle through which the will of the student was applied.

Students of the occult were required to perform additional tests prior to graduation that included a demonstration of the ability to kill an animal or a person through the power of incantation. One purpose of the test was to demonstrate that the student had the strength of personal will to actually act on what he had been taught. Tregear tells us that the student was required to kill a person who was close to him, someone other than a parent or sibling. Best suggests that the more closely related the killed person was to the student (specifically including parents or siblings), the more powerful a demonstration was made of the skill and knowledge of the student. In some cases where the priest may have been elderly or infirm, the teacher named himself as the student's target victim.

Tregear tells us that "one or more schools of astronomy" were located outside each important village. These schools were open every night, but no one was allowed to enter or leave, or to sleep there, during the hours when stars might be visible, from sundown to sunrise. Discussion at these schools centered on agriculture, hunting and fishing, and ways in which the constellations and stars regulated these activities. In villages where no such school existed, a house was designated as the Whare Mata. Among other meanings, the Maori word *mata* can imply the notions of observing objects (such as the stars) and acquiring knowledge.[20]

16 Maori Concepts of the Priesthood and Sacred Spots

For Tregear, the hierarchy of Maori priesthood began with the elite class of priests previously mentioned, called the ariki. This term (which Tregear says means "Lord") referred to a kind of priest-chief, comparable to the Arou Priest of the Dogon culture.[1] Although Budge offers no definition of the term, *ariki* may be a possible correlate to the Egyptian title *arq-heh,* a word that can be interpreted symbolically to read "comes to be the foremost of the earthly multitude."[2] Conceptually, the ariki priest was understood to be "the eldest son of the eldest son of the eldest son" and so outwardly embodied the title of *firstborn.* Next in the rankings of the Maori priesthood came close relatives of the ariki, followed by various other classes of priests of descending stature. As is true for the Dogon culture, Maori priests were an intimate part of everyday village life and so came to be associated with many different aspects of Maori society. Among other functions, priests and priestly knowledge played an important role in the processes of Maori agriculture, in agriculturally related astronomy, in divination, in the instruction of occult lore, and in numerous other aspects of Maori life.

Best asserts that the generalized term for a priest in the Maori culture was *tohunga.*[3] By more literal definition, the word *tohunga* refers to "an expert" and can properly be applied to an accomplished person in any field of endeavor. The word derives from a phonetic root *tohu,* which means "mark," "sign," or "proof."[4] Likewise, the term carries with it the implication of a *mnemonic,* which is a kind of symbolic aid to memory that characterized the ancient oral instructional tradition in cultures like the Dogon. For Tregear, the word *tohu* refers to "anything serving as a reminder; a token of remembrance." The term can also mean "priest" or "wizard" and so implies the *instructional* and *occult* aspects of ancient priesthood. The village tohunga was a respected person who was responsible for all the important ritual ceremonies that occurred within the auspices of a village.

According to Best, because of the lack of formalized temples or of an institutionally organized priestly structure within the Maori culture, each village priest was free to conduct his ceremonies with a fairly high degree of personal artistic latitude. Consequently, in the modern day, we find a range of differences in Maori practices as they have come down to us from region to region.

Best says that although Maori women could be trained as intermediate-level priests, they were almost never found among the highest classes of priests. Oftentimes, it was the women of the Maori culture who played the role of spiritual mediums and so were responsible for maintaining connections with the feminine energy of the nonmaterial realm. Yet there were still certain key rituals in the Maori culture that remained closely associated with elderly priestesses and so perhaps reflected the lingering influence of an earlier matriarchal era.

The term *Tohunga,* in this case serving as a title granted to a specific person, is both a phonetic and conceptual correlate to similar terms found in other cultures we have studied. For example, in the Dogon culture the comparable role of a knowledgeable priestly elder was assigned to a Hogon priest. Like the Tohungas, the Hogon priests were the keepers of esoteric knowledge. We have said that in the archaic matriarchal Sakti Cult, esoteric knowledge was the domain of priestesses of fertility called Yoginis. In Judaism, the likely correlation was to the Cohane priestly class. For the ancient Egyptians, the phonetic root *teh* and the term *tehen* (the actual pronounced vowel sounds are uncertain) were used to refer to a person of prominence. As an example, the Egyptian word *tehnu* referred to "one who has been appointed head."[5]

Much as modern society has seen a proliferation of "experts" in various fields, Best tells us that there also came to be many different grades of tohunga within Maori society. The highest-ranking class of priests were referred to by the term *tohunga ahurewa*.[6] Although a hereditary priestly class existed among the Maori, as in other traditions like the Jewish Cohane, any given individual who was born into that class might or might not choose to follow the profession, depending on his or her own particular inclinations and skills. According to Best, there was no particular style of dress or outward mark that could be used to uniquely distinguish a priest from any other Maori tribesperson. However, as a general rule, those who became successful candidates for the priesthood were understood to be among the most intelligent and capable tribe members of the Maori. This trend in favor of an intellectual priesthood was in keeping with yet another meaning for the word *tohunga,* which referred to "the soul or intelligent spirit of a human being."[7]

Maori priests maintained a very informal and personal relationship with village life that seems comparable to what we see in the Dogon culture, one that did not express itself in relation to formalized places of worship. In *Maori Religion and Mythology,* Best writes, "The student of Maori lore looks in vain for any evidence of the use of temples, altars, or any elaborate or permanent erection used in connection with religious ceremonial in former times."[8] Notwithstanding this statement, Best makes many references to informal places of worship that include such ritual objects as altar stones. He quotes Captain James Cook as having said of the Maori, "They have no such thing as . . . places of public worship; nor do they ever assemble together with this view."[9] Best asserts that no form of building was ever erected by the Maori to serve as a temple. Rather, the culture recognized certain sacred spots or places, called *tuahu,* which often remained unmarked in any overt way, or which (after the style of the archaic era of the cosmological tradition) simply merited the placement of several unworked stones. This symbolic approach comes out of the same apparent mind-set as the *standing stones, three-stone cairns,* and *dolmens* that characterized the Sakti Cult and that are evident in the Dogon tradition. The Maori word *tu* means "to stand," while the word *tua* is associated with the power of deities.[10] A similar Egyptian word *tua* can mean "pillar" or "support," and so from a conceptual standpoint it goes hand in hand with the notion of a *standing stone.*

In much the same way that we interpret the carved images of animals at Gobekli Tepe to have represented a kind of protowriting (later Egyptian names for these animals were pronounced like important terms of cosmology), so a standing stone known as a tua could effectively label a sacred site, referred to as a tuahu. Another Egyptian word *tua* means "to petition" but can also mean "to honor," "to praise," "to address," or "to pray."[11] From our perspective, the concept of *supplication* or *prayer* is characteristic of later ancient traditions and is not emphasized in the archaic forms of the cosmology. Where the concept of *prayer* is seen in later traditions, we find the notion of *celebration* in many of the earlier ones.

Meanwhile, appropriate to all of these meanings, the Dogon word *tu* refers to a "ceremony at which many people assemble."[12] One specific example that is given in the Dogon dictionary to illustrate the concept is that of a funeral. Similarly, the Maori word *tuakai* is a name for "an ancient burial place." According to Best, the Maori word *pouahu* "seems to be equivalent to *tuahu,* but is of restricted use."[13] The notion of a funeral again seems appropriate to the word from an Egyptian perspective, since the Egyptian term for the Underworld, to which the soul of the deceased person was thought to travel, was *Tuat.*

Best notes that the Tohunga played the role of a doctor in Maori society.[14] Similarly, Griaule and Dieterlen relate in *The Pale Fox* that the Hogon priests of the Dogon had broad knowledge of (and facility with) the medicinal aspects of the range of plants that grow within the area around the Dogon villages. Such knowledge would seem to go hand in hand with a tribal class who were scientifically aware.

In addition to all of these, there was a lower class of tohunga who were seen as general practitioners and were not considered to be very important persons in the community. These included a variety of shamans, seers, diviners, astrologers, and so on, whose powers of second sight and exorcism afforded them some degree of influence in Maori society.

According to Best, when a young man entered into the school of learning in order to qualify for the priesthood, he was referred to by the term *pia,* which means "beginner." The word *pia* comes from a Maori root *pi,* which refers to "the young of birds."[15] A comparable ancient Egyptian term *pa* or *pai* means "to fly" and is the root of a word *pait,* which means "feathered fowl" or "birds."[16] When the candidate then advanced an additional step to become what Best describes as an "acolyte," he was referred to by the term *tauira.*

17 Maori Myth of the Overturning of the Earth Mother

There is another set of mythic themes that hold significance across various eras of ancient cosmology that we have studied. From a cosmological perspective, these themes originate with an outlook on the egg-of-the-world (defined by the Dogon as the first finished structure of matter) where it is characterized by the spiral that can inscribe its seven starlike rays. Scientifically speaking, the notion that a spiraling vortex might exist at every point in space-time is set forth in a controversial version of string theory called *torsion theory*. The torsion theory spirals are described as being akin to tiny whirlpools of water (with dynamics similar to those of a *black hole* in the macrocosm). The cumulative miniscule effects of these vortices are understood to account for the attractive force of gravity. From the Dogon perspective, these microcosmic vortices are conceptual correlates to a *stellar bubble* in the macrocosm, of which the spiral of Barnard's Loop can be taken as a localized example.

One metaphoric image that is given by the Dogon priests to convey the rotation of this spiral is that of a *capsizing boat,* the same essential concept that gave birth to the working title of the previous book of this series, *The Mystery of Skara Brae,* which was originally cast as *The Overthrown Boat.* In that book, we argued that the eight Neolithic houses clustered at Skara Brae on Orkney Island in Northern Scotland were meant to represent an alternate view of this same structure, associated with the eight chambers of the egg-of-the-world. Traditional researchers say that the etymology of the name *Skara Brae* is uncertain, as is the origin of the term *Scot,* which defines the name of Scotland itself. A comparable Egyptian phrase, *skher bari,* means "overthrown boat," while an Egyptian term, *skhet,* (which we take as a name for the egg-of-the-world), means "to turn upside down."[1] The skhet is the concept we believe was represented in Neolithic times by a series of megalithic structures on Orkney Island that reflect cosmological shapes.

Meanwhile, the familiar religious lore of many ancient societies begins with tales of a Great Flood. Likewise, some of these myths imply that high levels of culture may have been previously attained by humanity in remote ancient times but were then ultimately lost to the ravages of what some cultures describe as cyclical global destruction. One possible mechanism for a cycle of destruction of this type on a global scale could possibly lie with a change in the tilt angle of the axis of the Earth. Any significant shift in the axis of the Earth would likely cause the ice caps to melt, raise sea levels, wreak havoc with the Earth's climate and tectonics, and produce widespread flooding on a global scale. From a scientific perspective, certain anomalous evidence points to such shifts in eras past. Nonintuitive patterns of glaciation that seem to have occurred during the ice ages, the discovery of petrified primeval forests beneath the ice in Antarctica, and reports of Siberian mammoths that may have been quickly frozen at the time of their deaths would all seem to point to a rapid and significant change in the alignment of the axis of the Earth.

Given all of this, it seems significant that one Maori myth is dedicated to the notion of the Overturning of the Earth Mother. Best writes in *Maori Religion and Mythology:*

After the separation of Rangi and Papa, they were seen to be ever weeping and wailing for each other. All space was filled with clouds

and mist; the tears of Rangi fell ceaselessly—that is to say, the rain
. . . the offspring were much distressed. It was now resolved that the
Earth Mother be turned over with her face down to *Raro-henga,* the
underworld. With her went Ruaumoko, the last-born, who was still
suckling the Earth Mother. This Overturning of the Earth Mother
was known as the *hurihanga a Mataaho.* It seems to be sometimes
referred to as a flood.[2]

In the above passage, the term *raro* is given in the context of the
cosmological notion of an underworld. However, the Maori word *raro*
actually means "under side."[3] The word *henga* refers to the hull of a
canoe.[4] From this perspective, the combined term *Rarohenga* implies
the notion of an *overturned canoe.* A character mentioned in the myth,
Ruaumoko, is a Maori deity of earthquakes.[5]

Similarly, if we were to examine the phrase *hurihanga a Mataaho*
that defines the Overturning of the Earth Mother, we would see that
the Maori word *huri* means "to turn round" or "to turn over."[6] Tregear
tells us in his comparative Maori-Polynesian dictionary that the comparable Samoan term *hurihuri* means "to capsize."[7] He defines the Maori
term *hanga* as a "causative prefix" that refers to a thing that has been
made or accomplished.[8] (Tregear writes "prefix," but his examples illustrate it as a suffix.) The root *anga* means "in a certain direction" and
might possibly imply the meaning of "opposite."[9] Meanwhile, the Maori
term *mata* refers to "the face," but according to Tregear it can also refer
to an inanimate object, such as "the face of the earth."[10]

The Maori word *aho* means "string" or "line" or can also refer to
a "radiant light" (we infer "ray of light").[11] Within the context of the
ritual alignment of a Buddhist stupa, the *axis line* that delineates the
four cardinal points of the Earth is defined in relation to two *rays of
sunlight,* emitted by the sun at dawn and at dusk, and measured in relation to the shadows they cast of a vertical gnomon. Based on these definitions, we interpret the term *hurihanga a Mataaho* to mean "the act of
overturning of the line (or axis) of the face of the Earth." The word *aho*

can also mean "daylight" and so on one level might imply the notion of the "overturning of daylight." This meaning makes sense if we consider that a full reversal of the axis of the Earth would (as the ancient Egyptians claim to have experienced) cause the sun to "rise where it formerly set."

There is also an implicit relationship between the Maori term *ao* and the Hebrew word *aur,* found in the Book of Genesis in the phrase "Let there be light." In his discussion of the word *ao,* Tregear specifically cites the phrase "God called the day light."[12] Such references serve to affirm our association of the cosmological terms *aa* and *ao* with the Hebrew god Yah.

It is an interesting point that the Maori term *ao,* like the Egyptian word *ahau,* refers to "the barking of a dog." In prior volumes of this series and in chapter 11, we have discussed the symbolism of the *V* shape (<) that a dog's mouth forms as it opens to bark, along with its possible relationship to the expansion of space as matter forms.

Best adds that the term *hurihanga a Mataaho* also relates to concepts of a deluge, sometimes referred to as a flood. He writes that the Maori believe the Overturning of the Earth Mother caused the rough condition of the Earth's surface, referring to variances caused by hills, ranges, mountains, and valleys.

The episode in which the Earth Mother is overturned is also referred to as the time when Whiro descended to the underworld. The name *Whiro* is based on Maori roots that mean "to spin" or "to twist"[13] and so suggests that the episode might properly relate to the spinning of the Earth on its axis. The "last-born" character named Ruaumoko of the Maori myth, who was said to have been left with his mother at the time of her overturning, is intimately associated with volcanic fire and ash, as well as with earthquakes.[14] These effects represent likely consequences that might accrue from any significant change in the tilt of the Earth's axis.

The Overturning of the Earth Mother is understood to have come out of a contest between Tane (the Earth God) and Whiro (the concept of spinning). Best tells us that this struggle was an enduring one that "took place in all realms, on earth, in the heavens, in space, and in the waters."[15] The general name for this struggle was Te Paerangi. The Maori word *pae* refers to "the horizon."[16] The word *rangi* refers to "the sky."[17] The meaning of these Maori terms together would seem to comport with an outlook that the *overturning of the Earth Mother* might refer to an actual overturning of the planet.

As a counterpoint to this Maori myth, Best notes that the Maori spiritual lore of the altar, called *whare wananga,* does not support the same outlook—that one source in which a term seems to refer to a flood is counterposed by another, where the same term seems to refer to the god Io.[18] The difference in viewpoint within the Maori culture may be comparable to the one that has grown between traditional Jewish doctrine and that of the Kabbalists in modern Judaism. Many Dogon inner concepts relating to cosmological creation can be more readily seen today in the philosophies of Kabbalism than in traditional Judaism. For the Maori, the difference in viewpoint might also be reflective of the apparent reversals in symbolism that we perceive to have occurred in relation to the symbols, deities, and lore of various ancient cultures.

A second compelling mythic theme that we have pursued in recent volumes of this series and cited previously in this book is that of the notion of a *sleeping* or *awakening goddess.* This is imagery that is given in relation to the formation of matter, and it applies most specifically to an effect that is said to occur at the moment that the female and male energies of the nonmaterial and material universes come together to catalyze the processes of creation. Our discussion of the concept has been made primarily in relation to Hindu and Egyptian myths of the Seven Houses. We see overt evidence that this same outlook on creation also persisted in the Maori culture. Best directly relates his understanding that, in Maori belief, female and male principles underlie the processes of creation, and he interprets these principles as correlates to the Hindu concept.

In the Hindu version of the Parable of the Seven Houses, it is the goddess Devi who makes a visit to a series of seven houses at dawn. As she arrives at each house, she encounters a housewife who is in the process of performing a specific act. These acts can be interpreted to symbolically represent the seven stages in the formation of the Dogon egg-of-the-world. As Devi arrives at the first house, the housewife who lives there is just waking up. Metaphorically, the suggestion is that we might properly equate the initial stage of creation with an awakening.

The acts performed by the housewives within these seven houses in the Hindu parable can also be interpreted to represent a set of basic needs within the daily life of a person, and they are defined in relation to a Mother Goddess. Egyptian terms for these needs center on the phonetic root *nehet* and so suggest a possible origin for the name of the ancient Egyptian Mother Goddess Net (or Neith). Possible traces of this same symbolism can be seen in the Maori words *nehe,* meaning "ancient times," *nehe,* referring to "the rafters of a house," and *nehera,* defined as "the rumor of a thing done."[19]

Key terms used in the telling of the Hindu myth lead us to words in the Dogon and Egyptian languages for specific cosmological concepts. The phonetics of these words suggests that we should associate this initial act of awakening with the term *yah* (sometimes given as *aa* or *ao*), which also happens to be the name of the Hebrew god. Our interpretive process with these myths leads us to equate Yah with the faint glow of light that precedes the first appearance of the rising sun at dawn. It is this glow that enables a waking housewife to perceive images in the material world as she begins to open her eyes. Appropriate to this outlook, the Maori term for "dawn" is *ao,* and the word for "radiant light" is *aho.*[20] By comparison, in the Dogon culture, the processes that create the material universe are initiated by a mythological character named Ogo.

The Maori word "to awaken" is given as *whaka-ara* or *whaka-oro.* Again, Tregear defines the term *whaka* as "a causative prefix," which he remarks is "very probably a form of *hanga.*"[21] As a way to illustrate how the prefix is used, he cites the Maori word *atua* as meaning "deity," and *whaka-atua* as meaning "to deify." The Maori term *ara* means "to rise up," "to awaken," or "to give birth to."[22] We interpret the suffix *oro* as a variant of the Maori term *ora,* meaning "life,"[23] and *ori,* which means "to cause to wave to and fro" or "to cause to vibrate." Each of these meanings has pertinence to themes of creation as we understand them within the ancient system of cosmology.

Aspects of this metaphor that equate the emergence of matter to an awakening are apparent in both Hindu and Egyptian mythology, appear in the Egyptian Book of the Dead, and are reflected cosmologically in various architectural forms of the Dogon, on Orkney Island, on the island of Malta, and in other locales of cosmological significance. Best tells us that, in the Maori culture, the Earth Mother goddess is "always alluded to as being in a recumbent position," comparable to the traditional position of the sleeping goddess. One of the traditional Maori titles for the Earth Mother implies the meaning of "face upward."[24]

If we may take the concept of an awakening perception of reality as a cosmological metaphor for the formative processes of creation, then it makes sense that the notion of cyclical destruction might be cast in relation to a similar metaphor. From that perspective, the Maori word meaning "to destroy" is given as *whaka-ngaro.* The word *ngaro* can mean "concealed," "hidden," or "lost to sight."[25] In Hinduism, the term *Naga* refers to a class of semidivine serpentine mythical beings who support Vishnu, but who can also be destructive.

18 Tracks of the Peti and the Papae in New Zealand

In *The Mystery of Skara Brae,* during our discussions of Orkney Island and the Field of Arou, we cited evidence to suggest that, after a period of some six hundred years characterized by tranquility and peacefulness, the Peti (pygmies whom we believe to have been ancient teachers) and the Papae (clerics whom we associate with the Dogon priests) abruptly left Orkney Island. One question that remained unanswered pertains to the likely locale (or locales) to which they may have migrated. We discussed possible connections of the Peti to later cultures in the British Isles, linked through a group in Ireland called the *Tuatha Danaan* or *Tuatha de Danaan,* considered by some (through linguistic implications of their name and other reasons) to be a race of supernaturally gifted people.

The name *Tuatha de Danaan* is traditionally translated as the "People's Tribe" or "Followers" of the goddess Danu. Another Irish perspective on the term is that it means "tribe of the gods."[1] We see Danu as a likely surrogate of the Sakti Earth Mother Goddess Tana Penu and, through the auspices of later symbolic reversals, also of the Maori Earth God Tane. From that perspective, it seems sensible to test possible alternate definitions of the term *Tuatha de Danaan* against Maori word meanings.

As an immediate observation, we know that the Maori word *tua* (as the root of the word *atua*) can refer to the "gods" and so is in line with one definition of the name *Tuatha de Danaan.* However, it can also

131

refer to "a birth ritual, comparable to a naming ceremony."[2] Appropriate to that definition, the Maori word *tehe* means "circumcised."[3] Based on Maori definitions, the term *tua tehe* (as a correlate to the term *Tuatha de*) would mean "ritually circumcised" and would refer to a symbolic act that characterizes our cosmological tradition. Furthermore, the term *Tuatha de* was similarly applied by Irish monks to the Israelites, whom we also know were ritually circumcised. The more specific term *Tuatha de Danaan* was later adopted as a clarification to avoid unnecessary confusion between the Israelites and the mythical Irish tribe. Calame-Griaule lists no Dogon word for either "pygmy" or "dwarf." However, apparent associations between the Tuatha de Danaan and pygmies may be reflected in a Dogon word *adene,* which means "short." From this perspective, the term could be a possible correlate to the word *danaan.*

Irish myth holds that the Tuatha de Danaan were confronted and ultimately defeated in battle, then consigned (in some views) to the Underworld or (in others) to an unspecified mythical land across the Western Sea. They became known as the Aes Sidhe (more commonly known as the Sidhe (pronounced *shee*) or Siths, or "the people of the mounds," a term that refers to *fairy mounds.* These were rounded, dome-like stone structures covered with earth (earthen mounds) that typically featured low, squared entrances, so small that an average-sized modern person would be required to crawl through the opening, rather than walk through.

In light of the traditions that long existed in Scotland and Ireland regarding the notion of *fairies,* it is quite interesting that the Maori also held similar beliefs. Tregear states that the oldest traditions in New Zealand held that fairies were actually living on the islands when the Maori first arrived. These were classified into three groupings called the Nagati-Kura ("descendants of the Red One"), the Ngaki-Korako ("descendants of the Albino"), and the Ngati-Turehu ("descendants of the Dimly-Seen").[4] Tregear tells us that the outward appearance of the light-skinned fairies was such that the Maori, at the first arrival of the Europeans, presumed they must be related. Consequently, certain

Maori terms for objects associated with the Europeans include a pre-fix that means "fairy." Consonant with the fairy groupings defined by Tregear, David MacRitchie writes in *The Testimony of Tradition* that Irish fairies were also understood to exist in three varieties: "In some tales, they are fair, and beautiful in feature, and yellow-haired; in others they are swarthy in complexion and hair; and again, they are described as red-, or russet-haired."[5]

As an apparent counterpart to the question of the ultimate disposi-tion of the Peti and the Papae on Orkney Island, confusion also exists as to the ultimate origins of what the Maori consider to be their earliest ancestors. Best writes in his book *Tuhoe, the Children of the Mist,* "The ignorance of the [Maori], as to the origin of their principal ancestor, is a very strange thing to anyone acquainted with the way in which tradi-tions, history, genealogies, etc., etc., were preserved and orally transmit-ted from generation to generation by the Polynesians. It may be that the ancient history of the tribe was lost in some great disaster which overtook the people in past times, or possibly the tribe originated with a band of refugees who took possession of these savage wilds wherein to dwell in peace."[6]

In their book *Counterpoint in Maori Culture,* Allan and Louise Hanson cite a Maori myth (described as one of a large set of variant storylines) in which a tribal group called the Tainui had prepared a field for planting but were "unable to use it due to a precipitous departure."[7] This myth repeats events that we believe may have actually played out historically on Orkney Island at the time it was abandoned (circa 2600 BCE), under what appear to have been urgent circumstances. As mentioned, we associate the instructors at this sanctuary with the myth-ical (and ostensibly *nonmaterial*) Nummo teachers of the Dogon and their students, who as Dogon ancestor-priests would have been Black Africans. Appropriate to that outlook, the Maori word *tai* means "the other side" or "beyond,"[8] and the word *nui* refers to a "person of high rank."[9] In contrast to the instructional purpose we infer for Orkney Island, the Maori myth is expressed in relation to a parent and a child, rather than a teacher and a student. In the Maori myth, the departure from the mythic land was by canoe (called the *Tainui canoe*) and was ostensibly from the ancestral Maori homeland Hawaiki, and the destination was New Zealand. Mythic parallels to the events in the region of Orkney Island suggest the possibility that an earlier migration, prior to the celebrated one from Hawaiki, might have occurred—this one originating from Ireland.

The Maori term *Aotea* or *Aotearoa* represents an ancient name for New Zealand, although the derivation of the word is unknown. However, according to Tregear, it also represents the name of "the first circle of the Lower-World (*Papa*), as opposed to the Upper-World (*Rangi*)."[10]

Geographically speaking, the cosmological terms *Upper* and *Lower* could sensibly apply conceptually in this case to the Northern and Southern Hemispheres. Interestingly, words of the Faroese language of Orkney Island provide us with a similar construction. In Faroese, *ao* means "world,"[11] *tehea* means "which,"[12] and *raro* means "under."[13] From this perspective, the combined term *ao-tehea-raro* (Maori *aotearoa*) could be interpreted to mean "world which is under."

Tregear tells us that the Maori word *aotea* can be literally translated as "white day," as opposed to the concept of "dark night." However, from a cosmological perspective, we equate the term *ao* to the name of the Hebrew god Yah. In the Hindu fable of the Seven Houses, we interpreted Yah's declaration "Let there be light" as a command that effectively reawakens a sleeping Mother Goddess who is the symbol of the nonmaterial source from which material creation derives. We also know that both the Maori and Faroese terms *te* can mean "the."[14] From that perspective, the name *Aotearoa* can be interpreted as appropriately referring to "the reawakening of Arou." The suggestion is that those who made the long journey may have seen the migration as a kind of fresh start for their Orkney Island tradition.

From another perspective, we can look at the name *Aotearoa* as a compound of two terms. The first of these, *Aotea*, we have said is also taken as an ancient name for New Zealand. The same word was also the name of a mythic canoe in which some of the original Maori were said to have migrated to New Zealand. Given other Maori/Egyptian commonalities and realizing that the vowel sounds of Egyptian hieroglyphic words are uncertain, it seems credible that the word is a correlate to the Egyptian term *ata,* meaning "boat."[15] The second of the two terms, *aroa,* is a Maori/Polynesian word that implies the meaning "to turn face upward."[16] In combination, the words *aotea aroa* convey the meaning of "overturned boat," the same essential meaning that, in our view, also defined the name of Skara Brae on Orkney Island. Another outlook on the ancient name *Aotearoa* is that it relates much more directly to Orkney Island in its apparent cosmological/mythical role as the Field of Reeds. From this perspective, the term combines the ancient Egyptian word *aat-t,* meaning "field" or "meadow,"[17] with the term *aaru,* meaning "reeds."[18]

According to a Maori myth, at the time of this incident of migration, an ancestor of the Maori named Hotunui (meaning "to long for the nui," which refers to something great or large) left behind a wife who was pregnant. In the ancient creation traditions, the domed or hemispheric shape of a pregnant *womb* can be symbolic of a temple or sanctuary. Before leaving the agricultural field, Hotunui instructed his wife that, once the child was born, it should be named Maru-tuahu (if it was male) or Pare-tuahu (if it was female). The Maori term *maru* means "sheltered" or "sheltered from the wind,"[19] and the word *tuahu* means "sacred place." We noted in *The Mystery of Skara Brae* that wind is a characteristic feature of the climate on Orkney Island. The sheltered sacred place that we associate with the instructional sanctuary on Orkney Island is a cluster of nearby islands called the Faroe Islands. These islands feature numerous natural defensive features that include high, unapproachable cliffs, channels with multiple whirlpools, shallow shoals where boats may run aground, and frequent, intense, but oddly localized storms—all protective circumstances that could make these islands an ideal safe haven for a group of ancient teachers.

We have said that the Egyptian word *per-aa* means "pharaoh" (for Dogon-related tribes, *faro*) and originally referred to a place, not a person. Tregear defines a Maori word for "a shelter from wind" as *paruru*.[20] From this same interpretive perspective, the phonetically similar Maori word *pare* means "to turn aside" or "to ward off."[21] Based on the ways in which cosmological words have survived in comparative cultures, we understand the phonetic values *f* and *p* to have been interchangeable correlates of one another in various ancient languages, and so terms like *per-aa* and *faro* or *pharaoh* can be taken as cognates of one another. An associated Maori word *parua* refers to "the edge of a nest."[22] One Dogon cosmological metaphor that is applied to their *egg-of-the-world* is given in relation to the concept of a *nest*. This can be seen as consistent with the "egg" designation itself, which for a bird is often found in a nest. If we consider the symbolic structures on Orkney Island as a representation of this same symbolic nest, then the Faroe Islands can be reasonably said to rest at "the edge" of the nest. A related Maori word *parea* means "inverted."[23] Taken in the context of other Upper World and Lower World references, the terms *Maru-tuahu* and *Pare-tuahu* could refer to two sheltered sanctuaries, one in the Faroe Islands and one in New Zealand.

In support of these interpretations, the Maori word *turehu,* which might be seen as phonetically quite similar to the term *tuahu,* refers to a "fairy or any supernatural being."[24] In Northern Scotland, the concept of a *fairy* is one that we also associate, both phonetically and cosmologically, with the *Faroe Islands.* The word *ture,* which can be seen as a phonetic root of the word *turehu,* means "law," "rule," or "commandment" and so reflects notions of authority, such as we assign to the ancient teachers who may have taken shelter in the Faroe Islands. Likewise, in his dictionary entry, Tregear defines the word *turehu* as having come "from the other side of the ocean."

One version of the Maori myth of Hotunui includes an episode in which the son Maru-tuahu is able to locate and reunite with his father, who has been badly treated by the group he is living with. This version of the myth tells of the mass killing of the detractors of Hotunui by his son at a large feast.[25] The final departure that is inferred by archaeologists to have occurred on Orkney Island also involved a large community in which a great number of domesticated animals, not people, were killed, and the animals were subsequently eaten, presumably as an alternative to simply leaving them uncared for. One Egyptian word for "enemy" is given by Budge as *sab,* while the term for "cattle for sacrifice" is defined as *sben-t.*[26]

Maru-tuahu, whose name bears a phonetic resemblance to *Maori,* was said to have founded a Maori tribe called the Ngati-Maru, or "descendants of Maru."[27] Related words from a similar root can imply descendants of a high or royal bloodline. They can also imply the meaning of "magician," the same term that we believe was applied to the Nem or the Nummo teachers of the Dogon on Orkney Island. The word *Ngati* also bears a phonetic resemblance to the name of the mythical Naga serpents of India, whom we know were closely associated with the god Vishnu and therefore with the instructed knowledge in the Sakti Cult.

Tregear and other researchers of New Zealand cite broad bodies of evidence that seem to reflect the presence of pre-Maori inhabitants in New Zealand. The traditional view is that the Maori may have arrived at the islands around 1200 CE, but the departure event we describe for Orkney Island occurred thousands of years earlier, perhaps as early as 2600 BCE. By comparison, Irish myths regarding the Tuatha de Danaan were first written down by Christian monks in the early centuries CE, and so, if the myths describe events that are historic, those events would have occurred sometime during the intervening centuries.

In 1999, a New Zealand–raised Californian named Martin Doutre published a book on controversial aspects of pre-Maori archaeology, which he specifically tied to Celtic Ireland, called *Ancient Celtic New Zealand.* One section of the book focuses on an ancient population in New Zealand, which is referred to by the names *Turehu, Patu-Pai-Arehe,* or *Potu-Pakeha.* Doutre writes, "Certain of these peoples become an easy target for relegating to the realm of Maori mythology, due to descriptions, given that [they] speak of **individuals of small stature** [emphasis original]. These 'small' (Caucasoid Pygmy) people had other described qualities which make them sound elusive, mystical and fairy like. . . . I have been advised that the main body and thrust of my work will be discounted on the basis of my obvious lack of credibility in believing in 'fairies.'"[28]

Given the apparent correlations to the Peti on Orkney Island, whom we associate in ancient times with the term *arou*, or *aaru*, phonetic parallels to the term *Patu-Pai-Arehe*, a collective name for early tribes that populated New Zealand, seem suggestive. Along similar lines, and consistent with what we know to be true about the peaceful nature of the earliest inhabitants on Orkney Island, Best quotes an informant named Pio of Awa in his work *Tuhoe, the Children of the Mist:* "The original Maori people of *Aotea-roa* were a very peaceful folk. War, strife, quarrelling were brought hither by the people who came [in a later period] from Hawaiki."

The Patu-Pai-Arehe were also known by the alternate term *Turehu*. Doutre writes, "The Pre-Celtic people of Ireland, referred to in secular history as the 'Firbolgs,' seem to fit the description of the 'small stature' *Turehu*." These people are described in mythological tales such as the "Cet-Chat Maige Tuired" and in an early collection of poems and prose writings called *Lebor Gabála Érenn,* which ostensibly reports events of the early history of Ireland. In these accounts, the Firbolgs were described as the People of Nemed, a term that phonetically conjures the mythical Nummo teachers of the Dogon, whom we linked to the Peti on Orkney Island in *The Mystery of Skara Brae.* Some reports also exist of Turehu tribe members who were said to be of average stature. In Doutre's opinion, late-era evidence of these groups makes it difficult to sort out which pre-Maori group was which, or whether, as on Orkney Island, members of more than one group, perhaps closely associated with one another, might have been present. In accordance with that outlook, Doutre writes:

Besides the types of people already described, there are legends and oral traditions regarding a tall, possibly black African group who were adept "gardeners." These people are said to have been so skilled at their art that they could grow Kumera [a type of sweet potato], even in the permafrost locations of the South Island of New Zealand. Other authors have clearly shown linguistic links between the Maori language and ancient Eastern Libyan or Egyptian civilisations. I believe that much of the Maori language, customs and mythology were gleaned over several centuries from the earlier civilisation, before the era of hostility.[29]

Descriptions such as these from Doutre align well with what we know to be true of the Dogon, who have also shown themselves to be adept farmers, even under often difficult desert conditions in southern Mali. They are known for their ability to cultivate crops on small flat terraces of ground along an escarpment in Mali. Again, the phonetics of the Maori language helps provide possible links between Doutre's descriptions of agriculturally adept Black Africans and the Papae of Orkney Island, who were associated with their godlike teachers, the Peti. For example, Tregear tells us that the Maori word for sacred food that was prepared for the Maori High Priestess and eaten in religious ceremonies was referred to as *popoa*. This same food was given as a reward to an ariki priest after successful completion of his initiate's instruction.[30]

The Peti, whom we regard as the nonhuman teachers of the Dogon collective memory, are described in passages cited in *The Mystery of Skara Brae* as having been pygmies or dwarfs who were closely linked with sorcery. The name seemingly given to this group by the Dogon was *Nummo,* which may well relate to an Egyptian word *nem* or *nemma,* meaning "pygmy" or "dwarf."[31] A Maori word for "dwarf" is *tupepe.*[32] The prefix *tu* refers both to the name and notion of a god, while the suffix *pepe* recalls the name of the Papae on Orkney Island, whom we identify with the Dogon. Combined, the term *tupepe* could be seen to imply the notion of "god of the Papae" and so would be an appropriate term for the Peti. Likewise, the Maori word *tupe* means "to disable and make weak by means of a charm."[33]

19 Symbolism of the Seven Mythic Canoes of the Maori

One defining theme of Maori mythology centers on the memory of their first arrival in New Zealand by canoe in ancient times. Based on our experience interpreting myths of other ancient cultures it seems appropriate to characterize these myths as *quasi-historic*, meaning that the myths might possibly reflect actual historical events, might serve as a symbolic mask for references of cosmology, or, like the Dogon concept of the Field of the Arou Priest, might possibly be interpreted both historically *and* cosmologically.

According to surviving myths, the Maori people arrived in New Zealand in seven mythic canoes. To any researcher who is conversant with the numerology of ancient cosmology, the numbers seven and eight, when encountered in a mythic context, should strongly suggest meanings that relates to the processes of creation, which according to the Dogon tradition occurs in seven physical stages, followed by an eighth conceptual stage. One way of distinguishing symbolism that is cosmological from statements that are possibly historical is by comparing any special terms emphasized within the myth to words or phonetic values that have obvious cosmological meaning.

For the purposes of this interpretation, our source for information about the mythic arrival of the Maori by canoe comes from Sir George

Grey, an accomplished nineteenth-century soldier, explorer, and governor of both Australia and New Zealand, who carefully sought an understanding of the Maori culture, language, and mythic lore in his role as governor of the islands. Our reference is to his 1885 book *Polynesian Mythology and Ancient Traditional History of the New Zealand Race as Furnished by Their Priests and Chiefs.* During his discussion of Maori myths of the discovery of New Zealand, he includes a list of the Maori names of the seven mythical canoes.[1] A close examination of these names, in the context of other creational references we have explored in this series of volumes, strongly suggests that they represent seven sequential stages of the creation of matter.

Grey gives the name of what he describes as "the first canoe completed" as Arawa. From a phonetic perspective, this term combines the Maori word *ara,* meaning "to arise," "to awaken," or "to arouse,"[2] with the word *wa,* meaning "an interval of space."[3] A related term *wai,* from the same phonetic root, implies the concept of water or liquid.[4] The term calls to mind symbolism from the Hindu Parable of the Seven Houses, presented in *The Mystery of Skara Brae,* which defines the first stage of the creation of matter as an awakening. Both reflect the notion of an act of perception of matter in its conceptually dormant, wavelike state that initiates the formation of matter.

The name of Grey's second mythical canoe is given as Tainui. This name combines the Maori root *ta,* meaning "to strike,"[5] and the word *nui,* meaning "great" or "large."[6] The combined term implies the Polynesian sense of the word *tanui,* meaning "to increase," and upholds Dogon assertions that the perceived wave grows as it is next drawn upward.

The third mythical Maori canoe was called Matatua. The Maori word *mata* means "the face,"[7] and Tregear cites as a specific example "the face of the ocean" and so calls to mind the creational phrase from Genesis, "the face of the waters." In the Hindu myth of the Seven Houses, it is a sleeping housewife (by some interpretations, a sleeping goddess) who is awakened during the initial stages of creation.

Appropriate to those meanings, the Maori word *tua* is a term for "deity" or "infinity."[8]

The fourth canoe of the Maori myth is referred to as Takitumu. The Maori word *taki* means "to begin to speak,"[9] while the word *tumu* can refer to "a low sound."[10] In keeping with a Dogon metaphor that compares the stages of the creation of matter to the speaking of a Word, this term refers to the initial vibrations that are prerequisites both to the formation of particles of matter and to the vocalization of a word.

The fifth Maori canoe is assigned the three-part name Kura-hau-po. The Maori word *kura* means "to redden"[11] and in the parlance of the ancient cosmology implies the notion of *reeds,* which are symbolic of the concept of *existence.* From our perspective, a single reed defines the concept of "that which is," and two reeds in combination represent the concept of "existence." The Maori word *hau* means "wind,"[12] which is a cosmological term that is symbolic of *vibration.* The Maori and Dogon word *po,* along with the Egyptian word *pau,* represents the concept of matter, or more specifically in the Dogon sense, the atom. Based on these definitions, the combined term *Kura-hau-po* would refer to the "vibrating reeds (or perhaps threads) of matter."

The sixth of the mythical Maori canoes was called Toko-maru. The Maori word *toko* means "to stretch out,"[13] and the word *maru* refers to a sheltered space.[14] The cosmological implication of the term is that of the formation and expansion of *space.*

The last of the seven canoes was given the name Matawhaorua. According to Tregear, the Maori term *mata,* cited above as meaning "face" in the sense of "the face of the ocean," can also refer to "the surface of the earth." Within the context of the ancient cosmology, the term *earth* is symbolic of *mass.* On one level, the Maori word *wha* means "four," which is the number assigned to our material universe in the numerology of the Dogon tradition, perhaps reflective of three dimensions and time. However, the word also means "revealed," "disclosed," or "known."[15] The word *whao* means "to grasp," "to lay hold of," or "to put into a receptacle." *Rua* is a familiar cosmological term that refers again to "vibration" or "sound." For the Maori, the root *ru* means "earthquake."[16] Based on these definitions, the combined name *Matawhaorua* implies the concept of the emergences of mass as a kind of receptacle that encloses vibration. From a cosmological perspective, this is a description of the Dogon egg-of-the-world or of a Calabi-Yau space in string theory.

20 The Sacrifice of the Nummo

There is a complex cosmological theme that is central to a correct understanding of the Dogon tradition but has not been discussed previously in any book of this series. Griaule and Dieterlen include a chapter in their definitive Dogon study, *The Pale Fox,* titled "Sacrifice and Resurrection of the Nommo."[1] (Note that the Dogon terms *Nommo, Nomo,* and *Nummo* are used interchangeably to represent the same Dogon concept.) This cosmological theme centers on an outlook in which our material universe is seen to be an impure counterpart to its nonmaterial twin. The cause of the impurity stemmed originally from what was described as an incestuous act on the part of Ogo, a character who plays the role of *light* in the Dogon cosmological myths. As the storyline of the myth explains, Ogo mistakenly imagined that he could create a universe as perfect as Amma's and, in trying to do so, stole a square piece of Amma's placenta to create a second universe. Once it was created, Amma could not simply reintegrate this second universe into the first one because of its perceived impurity, nor did Amma want to merely abandon the second universe. So instead, the choice was made to try to atone for the flaw in the second universe by doing what would be necessary to effectively remedy its impurity.

Similar themes are found in other ancient traditions, including Kabbalism, where the perceived flaw was introduced to the material universe by Adam and Eve, through a choice they made to consummate their relationship too soon. Because of what are essentially described as differences in time frames between events that occurred during creation and those that happened within a material frame, the remedy to that impurity is described by the Kabbalists as one that will take approximately six thousand years to work its effect. The vehicle for the remedy in Kabbalism rests with the annual celebration of the High Holy Days, which take on the cosmological symbolism of stages of creation.

According to the Dogon myth, Ogo had a twin brother who, "being of the same essence as Ogo," felt that he shared a moral responsibility for his brother's act of thievery. Consequently, it fell to Ogo's twin (known as the *nommo semu*) to implement the necessary remedy. The Dogon word *semu* combines the prefix *se* (meaning "to have") and *mu* (implying the concept of "individuality"). The terms suggest a nonmaterial nommo who somehow became materially individualized, in the same sense that multiplicity arises from unity. Significantly, Calame-Griaule gives a Dogon word for "sacrifice" as *numo*.[2] A comparable Egyptian word, *nemit,* also means "sacrifice,"[3] and a symbolic reading of its glyphs can be rendered as "waves know the spiral of existence and perceive matter."

In support of this outlook, Griaule and Dieterlen outline a conceptual structure for the universes in their article titled "The Dogon" published in the 1954 book called *African Worlds.* A caveat to the article emphasizes that it is based on only partial knowledge of the Dogon esoteric system, whose meanings can evolve somewhat as an initiate gains more precise knowledge through more privileged status. From the perspective of the article, the universe consisted of an egg that surrounded two placentas, each of which was supposed to have contained two *nummos:* one male and one female. However, the impurity that afflicted the placenta of the material universe, fostered by Ogo's actions, left it with only one male "soul." Griaule and Dieterlen write, "Seeing this, *Amma* decided to send to earth the *Nommo* of the other half of the egg,"[4] referring to the placenta of the nonmaterial universe.

Griaule and Dieterlen write in *The Pale Fox,* "The sacrifice was a preparation for the descent on Earth of an ark containing the principles, agents, and material for the reorganization."[5] The underlying purpose of the reorganizational effort was to remedy the perceived impurity. The Dogon term *ark* is a designation that is applied to their stupa-like granary shrine, and one that we also associate with the megalithic sanctuaries at Gobekli Tepe and those on Orkney Island. The notion of a mythical ark that ultimately came to rest on a mountainside in the region of Mount Ararat (the same region where Gobekli Tepe is situated) following a global flood is one that is also supported biblically.

The sacrifice was also to allow for "the expansion throughout the universe of the power and forces possessed by the couple of *nomo anagonno,* who were to remain with [Amma] in the sky." The Dogon word *anagonno* combines the term *ana* (meaning "male")[6] and *gono* (meaning "to wrap around").[7] Within the mind-set of the cosmology, the fundamental component of matter, called the egg-of-the-world, consists of a spiral in which a feminine nonmaterial essence akin to light becomes entwined (or "wraps around") a masculine material substance to form a spiral. Based on evidence such as the pair of carved arms and hands that wrap around the end of a pillar at Gobekli Tepe, we see this "embrace" as a symbol for a real-world instructional effort carried out in archaic times at sites such as Gobekli Tepe, which is also conceived of as an embrace between the nonmaterial and material universes.

In the Dogon view, one purpose of this instructional effort was to "restore humanity to culture" by effectively raising us up from the level of hunter-gatherers to that of farmers. Similar concepts are reflected in the Maori word for "sacrifice," which is *hapainga.* According to Tregear, the same term also means "to lift up," "to elevate," "to take hold of," or "to take in the arms" (embrace).[8] In keeping with both the agricultural purpose of the Dogon instructed tradition and its symbolic association with *baskets,* the Maori term can also refer to "a small basket for cooked food."

In order to put these references into context, it makes sense here to briefly recap our emerging outlook on the history of the Dogon and their cultural memory of having received civilizing instruction in ancient times from a group of mythical teachers called the Nummo. In *The Mystery of Skara Brae,* we presented evidence, first reported by the earliest Scandinavian visitors to Orkney Island in Northern Scotland, to suggest that a group of "strange" pygmies (called the Peti) had lived there in close association with a group of average-sized clerics (called the Papae) in Neolithic times (circa 3200 BCE). This occurred in a setting that might well have served as an instructional sanctuary, perhaps similar in nature to a college campus. An Egyptian word for "pygmy" is given as *nem* or *nemma,* comparable to the Dogon term *nummo.* The clerics, who were described as being outwardly distinct from the Scandinavians, were also said to have always worn white, as is a typical practice among the Dogon.

Likewise, we demonstrated that the architectural plan of the first Neolithic houses at Skara Brae, which included what researchers there called "unique" features, was an outward match for a traditional Dogon stone house, based on a design that carries specific cosmological symbolism. The common architectural plan implies that knowledge of a similar cosmology also existed in Northern Scotland. Dogon cosmology offers a framework within which to understand a series of megalithic sites on Orkney Island, and locale names on the island that have no known etymology make sense in relation to Dogon and Egyptian words. The Orkney Island sites are understood to have been abandoned by around 2600 BCE, seemingly under urgent circumstances. Through myth, folklore, and a minimal set of historical records, we seem to trace at least some of these pygmies to Ireland by the late centuries CE, after which time they may have been permanently driven out. Similarly, the Dogon recall that after a period of time their Nummo teachers either chose to leave or were forced to leave—an event that is seen as a turning point for humanity.

Based on these references, the suggestion is that like other aspects of Dogon cosmology, the symbolic theme of the *sacrifice of the Nummo* might well have had a real-world parallel. If we allow the possibility that following the last ice age, in some way unknown to us, a nonmaterial intelligence somehow came to manifest itself in our material realm, the process of that manifestation might have allowed for only a one-way transition. From that perspective, the sacrifice made by the Nummo may have lay with the choice to consign themselves to life in the "impure" material realm, permanently abandoning their nonmaterial universe for humanity's benefit. Appropriate to this interpretation, the Maori term for "sacrifice," *hapainga,* can also mean "to carry you away to a place you do not wish to go."

In keeping with the ostensible mission of the Dogon Nummo teachers, the Maori term *hapainga* is based on the root *hapai,* which means "to lift up." A similar meaning might conceivably lie at the root of the name of the Egyptian god of the inundation, Hapy, whose symbolism as a deity was aligned to the annual rising of the Nile River. We see another possible association with the agricultural aspect of the ancient civilizing plan in the Maori term *hapara,* which means "spade."

As we might expect, the more generalized Dogon concept of sacrifice also centers on cosmological themes. The Dogon expression for "sacrifice" is given as *numo pugu* and is considered by Calame-Griaule to be "an ancient term used only by the elderly."[9] A similar ancient Egyptian word, *puga,* means "to divide," "to open," or "to be opened."[10] It combines the word *pu,* which can be interpreted symbolically to mean "space enfolded by time,"[11] and the word *ga,* meaning "to be deprived of something."[12] If we read the glyphs of the word symbolically, they can be interpreted to mean "the spiral of space deprived of the embrace of time." Conceptually, the notion of an *arrow of time* would not exist within the massless realm of the nonmaterial universe, since due to an implied quickness of the time frame that goes with less mass, all events there can be thought of as occurring simultaneously; in effect, we could say that the nonmaterial universe, which is characterized by an absence of mass, is "held in the embrace" of time and mass. Additional insights into possible implications of the meaning "to open" can be seen in the phonetically similar Maori word *poaha,* which means "to open" or "to appear."[13] If we were to base our interpretation on the meanings of the Maori word, the term *numo pugu* could convey a sense of the "Nummo who appeared."

Our initial insights into the meaning of the Dogon phrase *resurrection of the Nummo* come out of an examination of an Egyptian word for "resurrection," which Budge gives as *nehas-t.*[14] However, because the processes of creation are characterized by various ancient cultures as an *awakening,* it seems highly significant that the same word for "resurrection" can also mean "to awaken." The implication is that the numo pugu, who from our perspective may have been deprived of their nonmateriality, then made their appearance in the material realm through a process of materialization that, like the formation of matter itself, is described as an awakening. Similar meanings come together in the Dogon word for "to awaken," which is pronounced *yeme.* The word combines the term *ye,* which implies the notion of "a sacrifice offered to remedy a fault,"[15] and the term *me,* meaning "placenta."[16] We can link the Dogon word to these same cosmological concepts since, as a part of her dictionary entry for the word *me,* Calame-Griaule restates the Dogon symbolic outlook that the twin universes constituted two placentas.

This same mythic theme in which a character is said to be sacrificed and then regenerated in the material realm is one that is expressed in Buddhism in relation to the god Prajapati and the formation of the two universes. It can be seen to underlie the concept of a primordial *unity* that becomes the source of *multiplicity.* We see possible traces of it in the myths of India, in which the goddess Sati comes to be dismembered and have her body parts fall to earth, and in the very similar myth of the Egyptian god Osiris, whose body is dismembered, its pieces scattered, and then reconstituted. If we choose instead to interpret the word for an *awakening* as referring to a *resurrection,* then the theme arguably comes to encompass later events such as the crucifixion and resurrection of Christ in the Christian tradition.

21 Putting the Maori References in Context

In this volume we have seen how the Maori system of cosmology, rooted as it is in a relatively recent historical period, nevertheless contains cosmological words of many key prior eras. It is our conclusion that to find these words commingled within the Maori language implies that each era is likely to have had an ancestral influence on the Maori tradition.

In keeping with that outlook, there are a number of significant elements that Maori cosmology shares in common with the earliest era of the cosmology we have explored, that of Gobekli Tepe. These begin most obviously with the practice of placing standing stones to mark the locations of sanctuary spaces. In keeping with those practices, the multiple stone circles found at Gobekli Tepe give the appearance of the kind of remote instructional site for civilizing skills that is alluded to in the Dogon culture, that is hinted at and revered in the ancient Egyptian concept of a First Time, and that is expressly assigned to a mythical locale called Vulture Peak in the Buddhist tradition. They are also in keeping with the instructed tradition that characterizes Maori village life in a much later era.

Likewise, symbolism of the Gobekli Tepe site that, in our view, pertains on one level to the Hebrew god Yah serves as a conceptual link between two distant eras. We argued in *Point of Origin* that archaic word forms, including an Egyptian name for the region, which we read as Het Pet Ka Yah, tie the Gobekli Tepe site to Yah. It is recognized that Yah (Ao) also plays a pivotal role in Maori cosmology. It is also apparent that various passages from Maori lore, cited by commentators such as Best, are a close match for passages in the Book of Genesis. These bring overtness to correlations between the Maori god Ao and the Hebrew god Yah and, by association, the Gobekli Tepe site. Specific details of the Maori myth in which the Earth God Tane ascends to the "heavens" to retrieve *three baskets of knowledge* uphold the notion of an instructional mountaintop sanctuary comparable to Gobekli Tepe and may well refer to three carved basketlike figures that are prominently inscribed there. Two arms and hands, carved in relief, that embrace the end of a Gobekli Tepe pillar are consistent with a Maori cosmological outlook in which the processes of creation are described as an energetic embrace.

References from the epoch of the Sakti Cult, in a period following Gobekli Tepe, are also evident in Maori cosmology. However, in the historically late era of Maori cosmology, we see signs of many of the reversals in symbolism that we have cited in prior books of this series for other ancient cultures, and so pinpointing these references requires a certain flexibility of perspective. Perhaps the most obvious symbolic reversal is the transition from a predominantly matriarchal to a patriarchal orientation in the era following 3000 BCE. Consequently, symbolism we associated with goddesses in archaic times is often found linked to male gods of later cultures, including those of the Maori. For example, the Earth God Tane holds a place in Maori mythology (along with a phonetically similar name) that is quite comparable to that of the goddess Tana Penu of the Sakti Cult. Furthermore, certain references from the Maori myths imply that Tane was once treated as a goddess. In keeping with these same reversals in symbolism, Tane has come to represent what is described as the "masculine principle" of creation for the Maori, while Tana Penu symbolizes the opposing "feminine principle" in the Sakti Cult. Much like the Sakti goddess, Tane is associated with mountaintops and standing stones, as well as (somewhat counterintuitively for a male god, but in keeping with a Mother Goddess) concepts of fertility and the phases of the moon.

The significance of archaic elements of the cosmology in the Maori culture implies that an intimate historical connection existed between the Maori and the traditions of these prior eras. The evolution of language, in the form of cosmological words, provides us with one positive method for tracking those connections. Tregear notes the presence of foundational concepts of Hinduism among the Maori, but in the absence of any of the later outward trappings of Hinduism. He notes that Tamil artifacts have been found in New Zealand, but without any cultural references to later Hindu deities. The implication is that the Maori and the Hindu cultures each benefited from the influences of a common parent culture linked to the Tamil, during a historical era prior to Hinduism.

Tregear's observations of Tamil and Hindu influences in the Maori culture are consistent with the same likely path of transmission that we proposed for the Dogon and Buddhist cosmologies in *Point of Origin.* This path began in the region of the Fertile Crescent (now southeastern Turkey and western Iran) in the era of Gobekli Tepe (circa 10,000 BCE) and was carried forward in the Tamil culture. In our view, it descended through the Sakti Cult, whose influences came to pervade India and are understood to have been ancestral to the later Vedic, Buddhist, and Hindu traditions. However, at this point, evidence strongly suggests that the Maori cosmological tradition may have taken a divergent path from the later traditions of India, one that likely took it westward from the Fertile Crescent and into Europe. Although our cosmological studies thus far do not track a specific evolution for the Maori tradition beyond the Tamil (a likely topic for a future book in this series), we pick up the apparent trail again centuries later in a somewhat distant region.

During the Neolithic era of 3200 BCE, parallels between the Maori god Ao and the Hebrew god Yah again link us in important ways to the cosmology of Northern Scotland. On Orkney Island, emphasis was given to a god named El, who is widely seen as a surrogate, and whose name is perhaps a phonetic variant, of Yah. For instance, in ancient times the name *Beth El* ("House of El" or "House of God") was assigned to an important shrine in the North Kingdom of Jerusalem. The Neolithic village of Skara Brae was located on the Bay of Skaiil. In keeping with a perceived naming convention of the cosmology, we interpret the name of the bay to have been *Skhai El,* or "celebrates El." In a previous book called *The Mystery of Skara Brae,* we argued that like Gobekli Tepe, Orkney Island also constituted an instructional sanctuary for concepts of cosmology and agriculture during later Neolithic times and was associated with the terms *ar* and *arou.* Similar instructional academies are a known fixture of the Maori culture and are also arguably associated with the phonetic value *arou.* These Maori academies are said to have been named in honor of (and explicitly identified with) a revered ancient school of instruction located far to the east of the Maori homeland of New Zealand.

The Maori myth of the Overturning of the Earth Mother upholds symbolic elements we cited for Orkney Island in *The Mystery of Skara Brae.* In the mind-set of the cosmology, the concept of "overturning" may be a reference to a periodic tipping of the Earth's axis, of the sort that might possibly have brought the last ice age to an abrupt close. In support of this view, there is an explicit Egyptian tradition in which there were said to have been three occasions within the cultural memory of ancient Egypt when the sun "rose where it formerly set," terminology that might imply the tipping of the Earth's axis. Likewise, a star chart is preserved on the ceiling of a portico of the Egyptian temple of Dendera that somewhat counterintuitively depicts stars as they appear in the southern hemisphere (rather than those of the northern hemisphere). Likewise, certain Dogon cosmological references are given in relation to the four cardinal points, but with the directionality of north and south reversed, and so could reflect a reversal in the axis. In the ancient cosmology, the concept of "overturning" is conveyed symbolically with the image of a *capsized boat.* We argued that the name *Skara Brae* combines two Egyptian hieroglyphic words, *skher bari,* which also meant "overthrown boat."

Symbolic associations that the Maori make between *reeds* and the concept of *existence* are likely correlates to reed references that, for us, define the Orkney Island site. This symbolism is linked to Northern Scotland through commonalities with Dogon cosmology and is overtly expressed in the Egyptian term *Field of Reeds*. The series of ancient megalithic sites on Orkney Island that we see as symbolic of stages of creation were joined by an ancient road whose apparent destination was the agricultural field at Skara Brae. A similar field, associated with these same stages of creation in Dogon cosmology, was known as the Field of the Arou Priest. References such as these ultimately led us to the Egyptian concept of the Sekhet Aaru, or Field of Reeds, also known by the Greeks as the Elysian Fields, or perhaps the "Fields on the Island of El." Like the Dogon Field of the Arou Priest, the Egyptian and Greek terms were interpreted on two concurrent levels, first in relation to a concept of cosmology but also as a real-world locale. Ancient Greek descriptions of the geography and setting of the Elysian Fields are a consistent match for Orkney Island. Reed references similar to those of the Maori and Orkney Island can also be seen or inferred in other related cultures. For example, a symbolic construction that is often substituted for the name of Yah in written Hebrew texts consists of two Hebrew letters called yuds, which we see as correlates to two Egyptian *reedleaf glyphs,* or *reeds*. From the first myth of the arrival of the Maori in New Zealand, reeds arguably play a similar pivotal cosmological role.

Again, in keeping with the stated belief of many ancient cultures that civilizing skills, as a prerequisite to the establishment of agriculture, were imparted to humanity in ancient times, Orkney Island gives the outward appearance of an instructional sanctuary. Numerous excavations on the island testify that an advanced form of agriculture was practiced there, which implies that the first known agricultural kingships may also have been an outgrowth of deliberate instruction there. These kingships arose synchronously at around 3100 BCE in various regions of the world. Village schools of the Maori provide instruction in many of the same core civilizing skills that we associate with Orkney

Island. For the Maori, instruction in the arts of cosmology, agriculture, and astronomy are understood to have been patterned after skills taught at a sacred mythical locale set far to the east of New Zealand.

Symbolic references from one of these early agricultural kingships, ancient Egypt, are also evident in the Maori culture. Perhaps the most obvious of these is found in the celebration of Ra as the deified concept of the sun. However, relationships between Maori and Egyptian cultures can also be seen in the shared notion of *ka* as a concept of *transformation, nu* as a term for *water,* and the phoneme *akh* as a designation for *light.* Likewise, the cultures shared a common outlook on the concept of death and its relationship to a mythical Underworld. Another of these kingships from the 3100 BCE era was found in Ireland, which is located only a short distance to the south of Orkney Island. A third was found in ancient China, whose creation traditions we explored in a prior volume titled *China's Cosmological Prehistory.* In each of these widespread regions, the established kingships were associated symbolically with lions (or a close leonid species) and with Neolithic names formulated on the phoneme *ru,* which was an ancient Egyptian term for "lion."

Two groups of people, clerics called the Papae and pygmies called the Peti, were reported in early Scandinavian texts to have been living on Orkney Island. Although it is known that the Skara Brae site was ultimately abandoned by around 2600 BCE, it is not clear what ultimately became of the island's residents. Historical records from that era are virtually nonexistent, and the surviving textual references we do have originated in periods that are historically too late to have much real pertinence. However, the unusually small stature of the Peti allows us to follow a presumptive trail for them that seemingly leads southward into Scotland and Ireland. Interestingly, the Maori term *Peti* was the name of a mythical marine deity who was considered to be an ancestor of a Firstborn ariki priest named Paikea. According to Maori mythology, Paikea managed to make his way to New Zealand after a deluge-related disaster.[1]

Just across the waters to the north and west of Orkney Island are a group of islands known as the Faroe Islands, whose language is Faroese. Given the apparent importance of the term *Faroe* in the Orkney Island region, it seems likely that these Little People known as the Peti might have been at the root of the later *fairy* tradition in Scotland and Ireland. Comparable fairy references are also found in New Zealand, and that suggests a possible link between the dwarfs or pygmies in Ireland and the pre-Maori pygmies who reportedly inhabited New Zealand. Each group constructed dome-like hillocks from stones, covered them over with earth and grass, and outfitted them with entryways too low and narrow for comfortable access by an average-sized person. These structures, which are found throughout Ireland and are referred to as *fairy mounds,* are a match for similar ancient stone mounds found in New Zealand, which date to an era prior to the Maori immigration.

In Ireland, myths hold that groups whom we interpret to have been likely descendants of the Peti were attacked militarily and ultimately forced to leave. Depending on which myth we choose to believe, they were said either to have departed to the Underworld or else to have left by boat to sail across the Western Sea. Maori myths that present mirror-image perspectives to those in Ireland cite the arrival of an ancient group of pygmies in New Zealand from an unspecified distant locale, situated somewhere across the sea far to the east. One such group was known as the Patu-Pai-Arehe, or perhaps the "Good Peti of Arou." Another suggestive link to the fairy traditions of Ireland can be seen in the fact that the same Maori term *Patu-Pai-Arehe* also means "fairy."[2] Likewise, an ancient name for New Zealand, Aotearoa, defines it linguistically as "the first circle of the Lower World" and has a correlate term in the Faroese language. Further support for the notion of a hereditary link between Ireland and New Zealand is found in the architectural form of horseshoe-shaped stone structures that serve as village schools for the Maori. A large number of similar structures have been excavated throughout Ireland, where their functional purpose in ancient times has still yet to be determined.

Perhaps our clearest reference for comparison of Maori cosmological symbolism to practices on Orkney Island rests with the Dogon, many of whose cultural traditions also agree with known practices of early dynastic Egypt. These seem to be representative of ancient Egyptian traditions at around 3000 BCE, only a few hundred years after the establishment of Skara Brae. Similarities between Maori and Dogon practices support a view that the Maori came out of the same instructed tradition as the Dogon. Illustrative of this is the village-based institution of the Maori priesthood, which is structured like the Dogon priesthood and has as its focus an esoteric cosmology that is formulated and conveyed in the same ways as Dogon esoteric practices. Likewise, Maori cosmology includes key symbolic elements that are a match for those of the Dogon, such as the concept of the po. Similarly, many of the well-defined tapu practices of the Maori are also reflected in matching Dogon observances.

The broader system of cosmology that we trace to each of these ancient eras in Turkey, India, Scotland, Africa, and Egypt is couched in a specific set of themes, many of which are also clearly evident in the Maori culture. These begin with the notion of quasi-mythic ancestor-deities who are revered for having brought civilizing skills to the Maori. Such themes include the idea that creation is catalyzed by *an embrace between feminine and masculine principles,* conceptualized in relation to *nonmaterial and material energies. Water* is defined as the *primordial source of material creation,* which is understood to emerge in ascending stages that culminate with the *separation of earth and sky.* Maori cosmology reflects the same principles of *duality and the pairing of opposites* that typify other ancient creation traditions we have explored. Maori concepts such as that of the po extend to the same realms of scientific creation that we see reflected in the Dogon and Buddhist cosmologies. The way in which the notion of an Underworld is treated in Maori mythology is consistent with its familiar expression in ancient Egyptian lore. Themes of the cyclical growth and destruction of humanity, linked in various cultures to descriptive images of a capsized boat, are outwardly reflected in the Maori myth of the Overturning of the Earth Mother.

The Maori tradition also reflects specific symbolism that is central to our ancient cosmological tradition. For example, the Maori preserve many of the nonrepresentational elements that characterized the archaic era of the tradition, such as the placement of unadorned standing stones to mark instructional sites and the assignment of spiritual symbolism to animals, along with the belief that shamanic meaning can be interpreted through the actions of animals. Cosmological concepts, such as the complex notions of *earth and sky,* have been anthropomorphized and deified for the Maori in the same essential ways as in the ancient traditions of India and Egypt.

Much as the architectural form of a house provided us with conceptual linkage between the village of Skara Brae on Orkney Island and the structures of the Dogon, so the architectural forms of village schools and fairy mounds serve to link Scotland and Ireland to the Maori in New Zealand. Meanwhile, we see a kind of transitive property at work: what we can only surmise about the possibility of instructed agriculture and astronomy in Ireland, due to lack of surviving records, we can say with certainty about both the well-preserved Dogon culture and the well-explored culture of the Maori.

Meanwhile, we have seen hints that New Zealand may not have represented the only destination of relocation for the Peti after their centuries in Scotland and Ireland. For example, my friend and fellow researcher Gary David traces aspects of the Hopi culture in North America to New Zealand. Over the years I have also become aware of Hopi practices that would seem to link their culture to the creation tradition of the Dogon. There are suggestions that short-statured Inuit people may have been descendants of the Peti. Given the close connection between the Peti and the Dogon, it seems not unlikely that pygmy groups in Africa could also be related. Likewise, a somewhat confused set of references, complicated by Celtic influences, suggest possible associations between the Peti and the later Picts in eastern and northern Scotland and southward into England.

Symbolism as it is practiced in the Maori culture constitutes yet another signature of the cosmological tradition that we have been comparing. The resemblances of Maori symbolism to that of our cosmology present themselves on many different levels. Perhaps the most rudimentary symbolic associations to compare are those made between cosmological concepts and animals. So, knowing that a duck often represents the cosmological concept of space, it seems sensible that the Maori word for "space" is *are* and a word for "duck" is *parera*. Just as names for the dung beetle are expressed by the Dogon and Egyptian phonemes *ke* and *khe*, we aren't surprised that a Maori term for "beetle" is *kekreru*.

On one level, the cosmological symbolism of animals rests on a set of root phonemes that express specific well-defined cosmological concepts for which we have cited ongoing comparative examples throughout this text. Much like the Dogon and other cultures we have studied, these phonemes and concepts are combined to form compound words of more complex meaning. Knowing this allows us to parse the meanings of more complex Maori words by examining the root phonemes. As is characteristic of ancient cosmological terms as we understand them, Maori cosmological words reflect a predictive set of diverse meanings that can often be cited as a basis for correlation to other languages.

Maori cosmology centers on the same symbolic principles and themes as are reflected in other traditions we have studied. It is characterized by familiar principles of duality and the pairing of opposites. Creation is understood to be from water and is catalyzed by the coming together of feminine and masculine energies. The structures of matter emerge in a process that is defined as an *ascent* and is intimately associated with distinct conceptual *worlds*.

Among the cultures we have studied, the Dogon seem to have succeeded in most carefully preserving many of the original meanings of cosmological words, symbols, and practices. However, the Dogon culture combines influences that seem to have come together through several distinct migrational paths. Starting from the Fertile Crescent, we see evidence of one set of influences, perhaps beginning in the era of

10,000 BCE, that most likely moved due southward and into Egypt from the north and are associated with the goddess Neith. The Dogon cultural memory is that their tribal group migrated from the banks of a large lake far away in the east to the Niger River region sometime prior to 1500 CE. A second set of influences, centered on the Sakti goddesses, seem to have moved in a southeasterly direction from the Fertile Crescent into India, extending eastward as far as Australia. These influences then made their way west to Africa and northward, perhaps through Ethiopia and Nubia, into Egypt at Elephantine by around 4000 BCE. A third set of influences appear to have migrated toward the northwest from the Fertile Crescent and across Europe to the British Isles and Scandinavia, arriving in the Orkney Island region sometime prior to 3200 BCE.

However, based on the earliest Scandinavian reports, it seems that Dogon clerics (descendants of the initial migrations southward from the Gobekli Tepe region) may have also actively participated in instruction on Orkney Island in the era of 3200 BCE, alongside a group of Nummo (or pygmy) teachers. These two groups would have constituted the mysterious Papae and Peti, who were found commingled on Orkney Island. At 3100 BCE, we see suggestive evidence of Black African influences in relation to four regional agricultural kingships in Egypt, China, Ireland, and Peru. It is traditionally understood that the Na-Khi from Tibet and China were originally Black Africans; in those regions, the word *na* came to be synonymous with the concept of "black." Surviving images suggest that the first Egyptian pharaohs, such as Djedefre of the Fourth Dynasty, were Black Africans. There are reliable references to Black African influences in Scotland and Ireland at places like Caithness, as well as suggestions of them at South American sites such as Caral in Peru. A set of unexpectedly diverse DNA results in Northern Scotland argue for the presence there of people from North Africa and Egypt, as well as from other widespread regions of the world. This may be reflective of groups of local initiates were either trained alongside or instructed by knowledgeable Black Africans. These

Africans may have also served as priests, administrators, and advisors to help establish the first self-sustaining agricultural kingships. Each element of this theoretic scenario is upheld in the Maori culture and supported linguistically in the Maori language. In earliest New Zealand we find reports of sorcerer-like pygmies, agriculturally talented Black Africans, and priestly schools where an esoteric cosmology comparable to that of the Dogon astronomy and skills of agriculture were taught to initiates, known as the Firstborn.

In summary, the comparative evidence we see suggests that there may have been intimate connections in ancient times between the Orkney Islands of the Northern Hemisphere and the islands of New Zealand of the Southern Hemisphere. From the perspective of the ancient Egyptians, the term *Upper* referred to a southerly direction and *Lower* to a northerly one. The Sekhet Aaru, or Field of Reeds, which we associate with Orkney Island, was cast as an Underworld in the view of the ancient Egyptians and the Greeks. Even in the linguistic legacy of the Maori, the concept of an Underworld, characterized as an abyss, is given by the term *raro* (or *arou*). But by the early centuries CE, it was New Zealand that was perceived of as an Underworld, both in relation to its ancient name, Aotearoa (arguably formed on the suffix *arou*), and in what we see as the coordinated mythic views of Ireland and New Zealand.

From our historical vantage point we see the link between the two island groups principally as one of historical migration. However, given the significance of the principle of *duality* in ancient thought, the apparent global reach of ancient cosmological instruction, and the anthropologically stated preference of the Nummo teachers of the Dogon to always be near water, it seems conceivable that these two realms may have been proactively postured as conceptual counterparts to one another. In archaic times, when Dogon directional references (preserved to the present day) seem to have been given with the positions of north and south reversed and when star maps as they appeared in the Southern Hemisphere were seemingly preserved in ancient Egypt, the Sekhet Aaru on Orkney Island would have constituted a symbolic representation of the Underworld of darkness, while Aotearoa *(Aotea aroa/arou,* or "daylight Arou") may have originally represented the World Above. In later times, following the Maori-recalled Overturning of the Earth Mother, those roles may have come to be reversed. In support of this outlook, an Egyptian word *aat-t* means "field"[3] and *aaru* means "reeds," so like the Egyptian term *Sekhet Aaru,* the name *Aotearoa (aat-t aaru)* might well also imply a second "Field of Reeds." Such an interpretation would offer an excellent rationale for the Maori having referred to their instructional institution as the *School of Reeds.*

Notes

Chapter 1. Introduction to the Maori

1. Wilson, "History—Māori Arrival and Settlement."
2. Tregear, *The Aryan Maori*, 83.
3. Best, *Maori Religion and Mythology*, 1.
4. Hanson and Hanson, *Counterpoint in Maori Culture*, 3.
5. Best, *Maori Religion and Mythology*, 2.

Chapter 2. Historical Overview of the Esoteric Tradition

1. Shortland, *Maori Religion and Mythology*, 3.
2. Sholom, *Origins of the Kabbalah*, 30.

Chapter 3. Deities of the Maori Pantheon

1. Best, *Maori Religion and Mythology*, 88.
2. Tregear, *The Maori-Polynesian Comparative Dictionary*, 472b.
3. Tregear, *The Maori-Polynesian Comparative Dictionary*, 106a.
4. Best, *Maori Religion and Mythology*, 90.
5. Best, *Maori Religion and Mythology*, 95.
6. Best, *Maori Religion and Mythology*, 92.
7. Best, *Maori Religion and Mythology*, 93.
8. Best, *Maori Religion and Mythology*, 103.
9. Best, *Maori Religion and Mythology*, 103.
10. Tregear, *The Maori-Polynesian Comparative Dictionary*, 538b.
11. Best, *Maori Religion and Mythology*, 110.

12. Budge, *An Egyptian Hieroglyphic Dictionary*, 426b.

13. Best, *Maori Religion and Mythology*, 112.

14. Best, *Maori Religion and Mythology*, 113.

15. Tregear, *The Maori-Polynesian Comparative Dictionary*, 462b.

16. Tregear, *The Maori-Polynesian Comparative Dictionary*, 420b.

17. Best, *Maori Religion and Mythology*, 113.

18. Best, *Maori Religion and Mythology*, 113.

19. Best, *Maori Religion and Mythology*, 113.

20. Best, *Maori Religion and Mythology*, 115.

21. Best, *Maori Religion and Mythology*, 116.

22. Tregear, *The Maori-Polynesian Comparative Dictionary*, 429a.

23. Tregear, *The Maori-Polynesian Comparative Dictionary*, 589a.

24. Tregear, *The Maori-Polynesian Comparative Dictionary*, 249a.

25. Tregear, *The Maori-Polynesian Comparative Dictionary*, 420a.

26. Best, *Maori Religion and Mythology*, 117.

Chapter 4. Parallels to Dogon Cosmology

1. Best, *Maori Religion and Mythology*, 2.

2. Best, *Maori Religion and Mythology*, 17.

3. Best, *Maori Religion and Mythology*, 8.

4. Tregear, *The Maori Race*, 450.

5. Tregear, *The Maori Race*, 423.

6. Best, *Maori Religion and Mythology*, 18.

7. Best, *Maori Religion and Mythology*, 28.

8. Best, *Maori Religion and Mythology*, 85.

9. Tregear, *The Maori-Polynesian Comparative Dictionary*, 168a.

10. Best, *Maori Religion and Mythology*, 32.

11. Tregear, *The Maori-Polynesian Comparative Dictionary*, 169a.

12. Calame-Griaule, *Dictionnaire Dogon*, 160–68.

13. Best, *Maori Religion and Mythology*, 134.

14. Budge, *An Egyptian Hieroglyphic Dictionary*, 560a.

15. Tregear, *The Maori-Polynesian Comparative Dictionary*, 501a.

16. Best, *Maori Religion and Mythology*, 35.

17. Tregear, *The Maori-Polynesian Comparative Dictionary*, 544a.

18. Tregear, *The Maori-Polynesian Comparative Dictionary*, 541b.

19. Tregear, *The Maori-Polynesian Comparative Dictionary*, 540b.

20. Tregear, *The Maori-Polynesian Comparative Dictionary*, 540b.

21. Tregear, *The Maori-Polynesian Comparative Dictionary*, 541b.

22. Tregear, *The Maori-Polynesian Comparative Dictionary*, 543a.

23. Tregear, *The Maori-Polynesian Comparative Dictionary*, 443a.

24. Tregear, *The Maori-Polynesian Comparative Dictionary*, 525a.

25. Tregear, *The Maori-Polynesian Comparative Dictionary*, 272a.

26. Tregear, *The Maori-Polynesian Comparative Dictionary*, 430a.

27. Tregear, *The Maori-Polynesian Comparative Dictionary*, 429a.

28. Tregear, *The Maori-Polynesian Comparative Dictionary*, 429b.

29. Tregear, *The Maori-Polynesian Comparative Dictionary*, 430a.

30. Budge, *An Egyptian Hieroglyphic Dictionary*, 430b.

31. Tregear, *The Maori-Polynesian Comparative Dictionary*, 536b.

32. Tregear, *The Maori-Polynesian Comparative Dictionary*, 520a.

33. Tregear, *The Maori-Polynesian Comparative Dictionary*, 520a.

34. Calame-Griaule, *Dictionnaire Dogon*, 276.

35. Tregear, *The Maori-Polynesian Comparative Dictionary*, 603a.

36. Tregear, *The Maori-Polynesian Comparative Dictionary*, 603b.

37. Budge, *An Egyptian Hieroglyphic Dictionary*, 440a.

38. Tregear, *The Maori-Polynesian Comparative Dictionary*, 415a.

39. Tregear, *The Maori-Polynesian Comparative Dictionary*, 291b.

40. Calame-Griaule, *Dictionnaire Dogon*, 212.

41. Tregear, *The Maori-Polynesian Comparative Dictionary*, 626b.

42. Tregear, *The Maori-Polynesian Comparative Dictionary*, 623a.

43. Tregear, *The Maori-Polynesian Comparative Dictionary*, 596a.

44. Tregear, *The Maori-Polynesian Comparative Dictionary*, 596a.

45. Tregear, *The Maori-Polynesian Comparative Dictionary*, 109a.

46. Tregear, *The Maori-Polynesian Comparative Dictionary*, 89b.

47. Tregear, *The Maori-Polynesian Comparative Dictionary*, 514b.

48. Tregear, *The Maori-Polynesian Comparative Dictionary*, 656b.

49. Tregear, *The Maori-Polynesian Comparative Dictionary*, 95b.

50. Calame-Griaule, *Dictionnaire Dogon*, 228.

51. Best, *Maori Religion and Mythology*, 33.

52. Tregear, *The Maori-Polynesian Comparative Dictionary*, 342b.

53. Budge, *An Egyptian Hieroglyphic Dictionary*, 230b.

Chapter 5. Mythic Themes
of Maori Cosmology

1. Budge, *An Egyptian Hieroglyphic Dictionary*, 202b.
2. Tregear, *The Maori-Polynesian Comparative Dictionary*, 481b.
3. Calame-Griaule, *Dictionnaire Dogon*, 261.
4. Calame-Griaule, *Dictionnaire Dogon*, 283–84.
5. Tregear, *The Maori-Polynesian Comparative Dictionary*, 530a.
6. Best, *Maori Religion and Mythology*, 105.
7. Scranton, *China's Cosmological Prehistory*, chap. 4.
8. Tregear, *The Maori-Polynesian Comparative Dictionary*, 644b.
9. Tregear, *The Maori-Polynesian Comparative Dictionary*, 113ab.
10. Scranton, *Sacred Symbols of the Dogon*, 53.
11. Best, *Maori Religion and Mythology*, 244.

Chapter 6. Pre-Buddhist and
Hindu Influences on Maori Religion

1. Best, *Maori Religion and Mythology*, 33.
2. Tregear, *The Maori-Polynesian Comparative Dictionary*, 443a.
3. Tregear, *The Maori-Polynesian Comparative Dictionary*, 479b.
4. Tregear, *The Maori-Polynesian Comparative Dictionary*, 656b.
5. Tregear, *The Maori-Polynesian Comparative Dictionary*, 484a.
6. Tregear, *The Maori-Polynesian Comparative Dictionary*, 484b.
7. Tregear, *The Maori-Polynesian Comparative Dictionary*, 341b.
8. Tregear, *The Maori-Polynesian Comparative Dictionary*, 120a.

Chapter 7. Echoes of Gobekli Tepe
among the Maori

1. Tregear, *The Maori-Polynesian Comparative Dictionary*, 504b.
2. Tregear, *The Maori-Polynesian Comparative Dictionary*, 472b.
3. Tregear, *The Maori-Polynesian Comparative Dictionary*, 656a.
4. Best, "Maori Medical Lore," 215.
5. Calame-Griaule, *Dictionnaire Dogon*, 261.
6. Budge, *An Egyptian Hieroglyphic Dictionary*, 874b.

7. Calame-Griaule, *Dictionnaire Dogon*, 260.

8. Best, *Tuhoe*, 110.

9. Tregear, *The Maori-Polynesian Comparative Dictionary*, 18a.

10. Tregear, *The Maori-Polynesian Comparative Dictionary*, 23b.

11. Tregear, *The Maori-Polynesian Comparative Dictionary*, 167a.

Chapter 8. Maori and Tamil
Word Correlations

1. Tregear, *The Aryan Maori*, 89.

2. Tregear, *The Maori-Polynesian Comparative Dictionary*, 14a.

3. Tregear, *The Maori-Polynesian Comparative Dictionary*, 37a.

4. Tregear, *The Maori-Polynesian Comparative Dictionary*, 189b.

5. Tregear, *The Maori-Polynesian Comparative Dictionary*, 332b.

6. Tregear, *The Maori-Polynesian Comparative Dictionary*, 10a.

7. Tregear, *The Maori-Polynesian Comparative Dictionary*, 444–45.

8. Tregear, *The Maori-Polynesian Comparative Dictionary*, 439a.

9. Tregear, *The Maori-Polynesian Comparative Dictionary*, 644b.

10. Tregear, *The Maori-Polynesian Comparative Dictionary*, 633a.

11. Tregear, *The Maori-Polynesian Comparative Dictionary*, 606a.

12. Tregear, *The Maori-Polynesian Comparative Dictionary*, 4a.

13. Tregear, *The Maori-Polynesian Comparative Dictionary*, 657a.

14. Tregear, *The Maori-Polynesian Comparative Dictionary*, 301b.

15. Tregear, *The Maori-Polynesian Comparative Dictionary*, 334a.

16. Tregear, *The Maori-Polynesian Comparative Dictionary*, 344a.

17. Tregear, *The Maori-Polynesian Comparative Dictionary*, 483a.

18. Tregear, *The Maori-Polynesian Comparative Dictionary*, 556a.

19. Tregear, *The Maori-Polynesian Comparative Dictionary*, 257a.

20. Tregear, *The Maori-Polynesian Comparative Dictionary*, 528a.

Chapter 9. Evidence of the Sakti Cult
in Maori Culture

1. Best, *Maori Religion and Mythology*, 53.

2. Tregear, *The Maori-Polynesian Comparative Dictionary*, 461a.

3. Best, *Maori Religion and Mythology*, 81.

4. Best, *Maori Religion and Mythology*, 104.

5. Tregear, *The Maori-Polynesian Comparative Dictionary*, 461a.

6. Tregear, *The Maori-Polynesian Comparative Dictionary*, 591a.

Chapter 10. Symbolic Aspects of Ganesha in Maori Cosmology

1. Tregear, *The Maori-Polynesian Comparative Dictionary*, 641–42.

2. Tregear, *The Maori-Polynesian Comparative Dictionary*, 661b.

3. Tregear, *The Maori-Polynesian Comparative Dictionary*, 648b.

4. Tregear, *The Maori-Polynesian Comparative Dictionary*, 347a.

5. Tregear, *The Maori-Polynesian Comparative Dictionary*, 540b.

6. Tregear, *The Maori-Polynesian Comparative Dictionary*, 407a.

7. Tregear, *The Maori-Polynesian Comparative Dictionary*, 664b.

8. Best, *Maori Religion and Mythology*, 37.

9. Tregear, *The Maori-Polynesian Comparative Dictionary*, 540a.

10. Tregear, *The Maori-Polynesian Comparative Dictionary*, 220b.

11. Tregear, *The Maori-Polynesian Comparative Dictionary*, 570b.

12. Tregear, *The Maori-Polynesian Comparative Dictionary*, 483a.

13. Tregear, *The Maori-Polynesian Comparative Dictionary*, 480a.

14. Tregear, *The Maori-Polynesian Comparative Dictionary*, 479a.

15. Tregear, *The Maori-Polynesian Comparative Dictionary*, 407a.

16. Tregear, *The Maori-Polynesian Comparative Dictionary*, 407a.

17. Tregear, *The Maori-Polynesian Comparative Dictionary*, 664b.

18. Tregear, *The Maori-Polynesian Comparative Dictionary*, 650b.

19. Tregear, *The Maori-Polynesian Comparative Dictionary*, 426b–27a.

20. Tregear, *The Maori-Polynesian Comparative Dictionary*, 40a.

Chapter 11. Ancient Egyptian Word Correlations to the Maori

1. Tregear, *The Maori-Polynesian Comparative Dictionary*, 472b.

2. Calame-Griaule, *Dictionnaire Dogon*, 266.

3. Calame-Griaule, *Dictionnaire Dogon*, 231.

4. Budge, *An Egyptian Hieroglyphic Dictionary*, 877a.

5. Tregear, *The Maori-Polynesian Comparative Dictionary*, 383a.

6. Tregear, *The Maori-Polynesian Comparative Dictionary*, 386b.

7. Budge, *An Egyptian Hieroglyphic Dictionary*, 233b.

8. Tregear, *The Maori-Polynesian Comparative Dictionary*, 6–7.

9. Tregear, *The Maori-Polynesian Comparative Dictionary*, 80b.

10. Tregear, *The Maori-Polynesian Comparative Dictionary*, 461b.

11. Budge, *An Egyptian Hieroglyphic Dictionary*, 266b.

12. Tregear, *The Maori-Polynesian Comparative Dictionary*, 640b.

13. Tregear, *The Maori-Polynesian Comparative Dictionary*, 3a.

14. Budge, *An Egyptian Hieroglyphic Dictionary*, 17a.

15. Tregear, *The Maori-Polynesian Comparative Dictionary*, 110a.

16. Budge, *An Egyptian Hieroglyphic Dictionary*, 542–43.

17. Budge, *An Egyptian Hieroglyphic Dictionary*, 129a.

18. Tregear, *The Maori-Polynesian Comparative Dictionary*, 18a.

19. Tregear, *The Maori-Polynesian Comparative Dictionary*, 19a.

20. Tregear, *The Maori-Polynesian Comparative Dictionary*, 32b.

Chapter 12. Yah and Maori Concepts of Creation from Light

1. Budge, *An Egyptian Hieroglyphic Dictionary*, 53a.

2. Best, *Maori Religion and Mythology*, 93.

3. Tregear, *The Maori-Polynesian Comparative Dictionary*, 14a.

4. Best, *Maori Religion and Mythology*, 53.

5. Best, *Maori Religion and Mythology*, 53.

6. Tregear, *The Maori-Polynesian Comparative Dictionary*, 7a.

7. Tregear, *The Maori-Polynesian Comparative Dictionary*, 96b.

8. Tregear, *The Maori-Polynesian Comparative Dictionary*, 571b.

9. Tregear, *The Maori-Polynesian Comparative Dictionary*, 358b.

10. Tregear, *The Maori-Polynesian Comparative Dictionary*, 404a.

11. Tregear, *The Maori-Polynesian Comparative Dictionary*, 118b.

12. Tregear, *The Maori-Polynesian Comparative Dictionary*, 398b.

13. Tregear, *The Maori-Polynesian Comparative Dictionary*, 62a.

14. Tregear, *The Maori-Polynesian Comparative Dictionary*, 271a.

15. Tregear, *The Maori-Polynesian Comparative Dictionary*, 541a.

16. Best, *Maori Religion and Mythology*, 36.

17. Best, *Journal of the Polynesian Society* 16, 109.

18. Tregear, *The Maori-Polynesian Comparative Dictionary*, 14a.

19. Best, *Maori Religion and Mythology*, 100.

Chapter 13. Foundational Philosophies in Maori Cosmology

1. Calame-Griaule, *Dictionnaire Dogon*, 238.

2. Calame-Griaule, *Dictionnaire Dogon*, 147.

3. Budge, *An Egyptian Hieroglyphic Dictionary*, 634a.

4. Budge, *An Egyptian Hieroglyphic Dictionary*, 526b.

5. Tregear, *The Maori-Polynesian Comparative Dictionary*, 192a.

6. Hanson and Hanson, *Counterpoint in Maori Culture*, 19.

7. Hanson and Hanson, *Counterpoint in Maori Culture*, 20.

8. Hanson and Hanson, *Counterpoint in Maori Culture*, 23.

9. Hanson and Hanson, *Counterpoint in Maori Culture*, 25.

10. Hanson and Hanson, *Counterpoint in Maori Culture*, 19.

11. Hanson and Hanson, *Counterpoint in Maori Culture*, 30.

12. Hanson and Hanson, *Counterpoint in Maori Culture*, 72.

13. Hanson and Hanson, *Counterpoint in Maori Culture*, 49.

14. Hanson and Hanson, *Counterpoint in Maori Culture*, 44–45.

15. Hanson and Hanson, *Counterpoint in Maori Culture*, 48–49.

16. Tregear, *The Maori-Polynesian Comparative Dictionary*, 651a.

17. Saraswati, *Samkhya Darshan*, 65.

18. Tregear, *The Maori-Polynesian Comparative Dictionary*, 190a.

19. Tregear, *The Maori-Polynesian Comparative Dictionary*, 214b.

20. Saraswati, *Samkhya Darshan*, 63.

21. Tregear, *The Maori-Polynesian Comparative Dictionary*, 574a.

22. Tregear, *The Maori-Polynesian Comparative Dictionary*, 102a.

23. Budge, *An Egyptian Hieroglyphic Dictionary*, 557b.

Chapter 14. Maori References to the Field of Arou

1. Tregear, *The Maori-Polynesian Comparative Dictionary*, 24a.

2. Tregear, *The Maori-Polynesian Comparative Dictionary*, 52a.

3. Tregear, *The Maori-Polynesian Comparative Dictionary*, 5a.

4. Tregear, *The Maori-Polynesian Comparative Dictionary*, 18a.

5. Tregear, *The Maori-Polynesian Comparative Dictionary,* 613b.

6. Tregear, *The Maori-Polynesian Comparative Dictionary,* 56b.

7. Tregear, *The Maori-Polynesian Comparative Dictionary,* 257a.

8. Tregear, *The Maori-Polynesian Comparative Dictionary,* 612b.

9. Tregear, *The Maori-Polynesian Comparative Dictionary,* 185a.

10. Tregear, *The Maori-Polynesian Comparative Dictionary,* 334a.

11. Tregear, *The Maori-Polynesian Comparative Dictionary,* 297b.

Chapter 15. The Wharekura, or School of Reeds

1. Tregear, *The Maori Race,* 374.

2. Tregear, *The Maori-Polynesian Comparative Dictionary,* 196b.

3. Tregear, *The Maori-Polynesian Comparative Dictionary,* 455a.

4. Best, *Tuhoe,* 1096.

5. Calame-Griaule, *Dictionnaire Dogon,* 230.

6. Brighenti, *Sakti Cult in Orissa,* 35.

7. Tregear, *The Maori Race,* 376.

8. Tregear, *The Maori Race,* 374.

9. Denvir, "Fulachta Fiadh—An Irish Mystery," 12.

10. SCARF, "3.3.1 Burnt Mounds."

11. Ó Néill, *"Lapidibus in Igne Calefactis Coquebatur."*

12. Green, *World of Druids,* 14, 21.

13. Tregear, *The Maori-Polynesian Comparative Dictionary,* 335b.

14. Tregear, *The Maori-Polynesian Comparative Dictionary,* 612b.

15. Budge, *An Egyptian Hieroglyphic Dictionary,* 694b–95a.

16. Parker, *Webster's Faroese-English Thesaurus,* 65b.

17. Tregear, *The Maori Race,* 375.

18. Tregear, *The Maori Race,* 376.

19. Tregear, *The Maori Race,* 376–77.

20. Tregear, *The Maori-Polynesian Comparative Dictionary,* 220b.

Chapter 16. Maori Concepts of the Priesthood and Sacred Spots

1. Tregear, *The Maori Race,* 124.

2. Budge, *An Egyptian Hieroglyphic Dictionary,* 7b.

3. Best, *Maori Religion and Mythology,* 163.

4. Tregear, *The Maori-Polynesian Comparative Dictionary,* 524a.

5. Budge, *An Egyptian Hieroglyphic Dictionary,* 885b.

6. Best, *Maori Religion and Mythology,* 163.

7. Tregear, *The Maori-Polynesian Comparative Dictionary,* 524a.

8. Best, *Maori Religion and Mythology,* 170.

9. Best, *Maori Religion and Mythology,* 164.

10. Tregear, *The Maori-Polynesian Comparative Dictionary,* 540ab.

11. Budge, *An Egyptian Hieroglyphic Dictionary,* 824a.

12. Calame-Griaule, *Dictionnaire Dogon,* 289.

13. Best, *Maori Religion and Mythology,* 171.

14. Best, *Maori Religion and Mythology,* 163.

15. Tregear, *The Maori-Polynesian Comparative Dictionary,* 334b.

16. Budge, *An Egyptian Hieroglyphic Dictionary,* 230a.

Chapter 17. Maori Myth of the Overturning of the Earth Mother

1. Budge, *An Egyptian Hieroglyphic Dictionary,* 695a.

2. Best, *Maori Religion and Mythology,* 52.

3. Tregear, *The Maori-Polynesian Comparative Dictionary,* 398b.

4. Tregear, *The Maori-Polynesian Comparative Dictionary,* 62a.

5. Tregear, *The Maori-Polynesian Comparative Dictionary,* 432b.

6. Tregear, *The Maori-Polynesian Comparative Dictionary,* 95b.

7. Tregear, *The Maori-Polynesian Comparative Dictionary,* 95b.

8. Tregear, *The Maori-Polynesian Comparative Dictionary,* 46a.

9. Tregear, *The Maori-Polynesian Comparative Dictionary,* 12–13.

10. Tregear, *The Maori-Polynesian Comparative Dictionary,* 220b.

11. Tregear, *The Maori-Polynesian Comparative Dictionary,* 3b–4a.

12. Tregear, *The Maori-Polynesian Comparative Dictionary,* 15a.

13. Tregear, *The Maori-Polynesian Comparative Dictionary,* 625a.

14. Best, *Maori Religion and Mythology,* 70.

15. Best, *Maori Religion and Mythology,* 71.

16. Tregear, *The Maori-Polynesian Comparative Dictionary,* 297b.

17. Tregear, *The Maori-Polynesian Comparative Dictionary,* 392b.

18. Best, *Maori Religion and Mythology,* 52.

19. Tregear, *The Maori-Polynesian Comparative Dictionary*, 264b–65a.

20. Tregear, *The Maori-Polynesian Comparative Dictionary*, 14a.

21. Tregear, *The Maori-Polynesian Comparative Dictionary*, 606a.

22. Tregear, *The Maori-Polynesian Comparative Dictionary*, 18a.

23. Tregear, *The Maori-Polynesian Comparative Dictionary*, 292b.

24. Best, *Maori Religion and Mythology*, 53.

25. Tregear, *The Maori-Polynesian Comparative Dictionary*, 278b.

Chapter 18. Tracks of the Peti and the Papae in New Zealand

1. Koch, *Celtic Culture*, 1693–94.

2. Tregear, *The Maori-Polynesian Comparative Dictionary*, 541b.

3. Tregear, *The Maori-Polynesian Comparative Dictionary*, 502a, 634b.

4. Tregear, *Maori Race*, 524.

5. MacRitchie, *The Testimony of Tradition*, 156.

6. Best, *Tuhoe*, 21.

7. Hanson and Hanson, *Counterpoint in Maori Culture*, 27.

8. Tregear, *The Maori-Polynesian Comparative Dictionary*, 446b.

9. Tregear, *The Maori-Polynesian Comparative Dictionary*, 271a.

10. Tregear, *The Maori-Polynesian Comparative Dictionary*, 15b.

11. Tregear, *The Maori-Polynesian Comparative Dictionary*, 665a.

12. Tregear, *The Maori-Polynesian Comparative Dictionary*, 502b.

13. Tregear, *The Maori-Polynesian Comparative Dictionary*, 663a.

14. Tregear, *The Maori-Polynesian Comparative Dictionary*, 501a.

15. Budge, *An Egyptian Hieroglyphic Dictionary*, 13a.

16. Tregear, *The Maori-Polynesian Comparative Dictionary*, 24ab.

17. Budge, *An Egyptian Hieroglyphic Dictionary*, 27a.

18. Budge, *An Egyptian Hieroglyphic Dictionary*, 21b.

19. Tregear, *The Maori-Polynesian Comparative Dictionary*, 218b.

20. Tregear, *The Maori-Polynesian Comparative Dictionary*, 324b.

21. Tregear, *The Maori-Polynesian Comparative Dictionary*, 321b.

22. Tregear, *The Maori-Polynesian Comparative Dictionary*, 324b.

23. Tregear, *The Maori-Polynesian Comparative Dictionary*, 321b.

24. Tregear, *The Maori-Polynesian Comparative Dictionary*, 562a.

25. Hanson and Hanson, *Counterpoint in Maori Culture*, 27.

26. Budge, *An Egyptian Hieroglyphic Dictionary*, 642a, 658a.
27. Tregear, *The Maori-Polynesian Comparative Dictionary*, 280b.
28. Doutre, *Ancient Celtic New Zealand*, 53.
29. Doutre, *Ancient Celtic New Zealand*, 56.
30. Tregear, *Maori Race*, 423; and Tregear, *The Maori-Polynesian Comparative Dictionary*, 343b.
31. Budge, *Egyptian Hieroglyphic Dictionary*, 374b.
32. Tregear, *The Maori-Polynesian Comparative Dictionary*, 555b.
33. Tregear, *The Maori-Polynesian Comparative Dictionary*, 555b.

Chapter 19. Symbolism of the Seven Mythic Canoes of the Maori

1. Grey, *Polynesian Mythology*, 83.
2. Tregear, *The Maori-Polynesian Comparative Dictionary*, 18a.
3. Tregear, *The Maori-Polynesian Comparative Dictionary*, 583a.
4. Tregear, *The Maori-Polynesian Comparative Dictionary*, 589a.
5. Tregear, *The Maori-Polynesian Comparative Dictionary*, 446b.
6. Tregear, *The Maori-Polynesian Comparative Dictionary*, 271a.
7. Tregear, *The Maori-Polynesian Comparative Dictionary*, 220b.
8. Tregear, *The Maori-Polynesian Comparative Dictionary*, 540b.
9. Tregear, *The Maori-Polynesian Comparative Dictionary*, 453b.
10. Tregear, *The Maori-Polynesian Comparative Dictionary*, 551a.
11. Tregear, *The Maori-Polynesian Comparative Dictionary*, 185a.
12. Tregear, *The Maori-Polynesian Comparative Dictionary*, 52a.
13. Tregear, *The Maori-Polynesian Comparative Dictionary*, 528a.
14. Tregear, *The Maori-Polynesian Comparative Dictionary*, 218–19.
15. Tregear, *The Maori-Polynesian Comparative Dictionary*, 603a.
16. Tregear, *The Maori-Polynesian Comparative Dictionary*, 429–30.

Chapter 20. The Sacrifice of the Nummo

1. Griaule and Dieterlen, *The Pale Fox*, chap. 3.
2. Calame-Griaule, *Dictionnaire Dogon*, 327.
3. Budge, *An Egyptian Hieroglyphic Dictionary*, 373b.
4. Griaule and Dieterlen, "The Dogon," 86.

5. Griaule and Dieterlen, *The Pale Fox,* 248.

6. Calame-Griaule, *Dictionnaire Dogon,* 7.

7. Calame-Griaule, *Dictionnaire Dogon,* 106.

8. Tregear, *The Maori-Polynesian Comparative Dictionary,* 655b, 48a.

9. Calame-Griaule, *Dictionnaire Dogon,* 204.

10. Budge, *An Egyptian Hieroglyphic Dictionary,* 235a.

11. Budge, *An Egyptian Hieroglyphic Dictionary,* 234b.

12. Budge, *An Egyptian Hieroglyphic Dictionary,* 800.

13. Tregear, *The Maori-Polynesian Comparative Dictionary,* 344a.

14. Budge, *An Egyptian Hieroglyphic Dictionary,* 381a.

15. Calame-Griaule, *Dictionnaire Dogon,* 308.

16. Calame-Griaule, *Dictionnaire Dogon,* 185.

Chapter 21. Putting the Maori References in Context

1. Tregear, *The Maori-Polynesian Comparative Dictionary,* 334a, 303a.

2. Tregear, *The Maori-Polynesian Comparative Dictionary,* 328b, 640b.

3. Budge, *An Egyptian Hieroglyphic Dictionary,* 27a.

Bibliography

Best, Elsdon. "Maori Medical Lore." *Journal of the Polynesian Society* 13 (1904).

———. *Journal of the Polynesian Society* 16.

———. *Maori Religion and Mythology.* Wellington, New Zealand: W. A. G. Skinner, Government Printer, 1924.

———. *Tuhoe, the Children of the Mist: A Sketch of the Origin, History, Myths, and Beliefs of the Tuhoe Tribe of the Maori of New Zealand; With Some Account of Other Early Tribes of the Bay of Plenty District.* Wellington, New Zealand. 1st ed. The Board of Maori Ethnological Research, 1925.

Brighenti, Francesco. *Sakti Cult in Orissa.* New Delhi, India: D. K. Printworld (P) Ltd., 1963.

Budge, E. A. Wallis. *An Egyptian Hieroglyphic Dictionary.* New York: Dover, 1978.

Calame-Griaule, Genevieve. *Dictionnaire Dogon.* Paris: Librarie C. Klincksieck, 1968.

Denvir, Anne-Marie. "Fulachta Fiadh—An Irish Mystery." Undergraduate diss., the Queen's University of Belfast, 1999.

Doutre, Martin. *Ancient Celtic New Zealand.* Auckland, New Zealand: De Danann Publishers, 1999.

Forde, Daryll, ed. *African Worlds: Studies in the Cosmological Ideas and Social Values of African Peoples.* London: Oxford University Press, 1954.

Frazer, J. *The Battle of Moytura: The First Battle of the Mag Tuired.* Middletown, Del.: Theophania Publishing, 2015.

Granoff, Phyllis. "Ganeśa as Metaphor: The Mudgala Purāna." In *Ganesh: Studies of an Asian God,* edited by Robert L. Brown, 85–100. Delhi, India: Sri Satguru Publications, 1991.

Green, Miranda J. *The World of Druids.* 3rd ed. London: Thames & Hudson, 2005.

Grey, Sir George. *Polynesian Mythology and Ancient Traditional History of the*

New Zealand Race as Furnished by Their Priests and Chiefs. Middletown, Del.: Adamant Media Corporation, 2005.

Griaule, Marcel. *Conversations with Ogotemmeli.* London: Oxford University Press, 1970.

Griaule, Marcel, and Germaine Dieterlen. "The Dogon." In *African Worlds: Studies in the Cosmological Ideas and Social Values of African Peoples,* edited by Daryll Forde, 83–110. London: Oxford University Press, 1954.

———. *The Pale Fox.* Paris: Continuum Foundation, 1986. First published in French as *Le renard pale,* Paris: l'Intitut d'Ethnologie, 1965.

Hanson, F. Allan, and Louise Hanson. *Counterpoint in Maori Culture.* London: Routledge & Kegan Paul, 1983.

Hochstetter, Ferdinand von, Dr. *New Zealand: Its Physical Geography, Geology, and Natural History; With Special Reference to the Results of Government Expeditions in the Provinces of Auckland and Nelson.* Stuttgart, Germany: J. G. Cotta, 1867.

Howe, Kerry. "Ideas of Maori Origins." Te Ara—The Encyclopedia of New Zealand (online). www.TeAra.govt.nz/en/ideas-of-maori-origins.

Koch, John T., Ph.D., ed. *Celtic Culture: A Historical Encyclopedia.* Santa Barbara, Calif.: ABC-CLIO, 2005.

MacRitchie, David. *The Testimony of Tradition.* London: Kegan Paul, Trench, Trubner & Co. Limited, 1890.

Ó Néill, J. *"Lapidibus in Igne Calefactis Coquebatur:* The Historical Burnt Mound Tradition." *Journal of Irish Archaeology* XII/XIII (2004): 79–85.

Parker, Philip M. *Webster's Faroese-English Thesaurus Dictionary.* San Diego, Calif.: ICON Classics, 2008.

Saraswati, Swami Niranjanananda. *Samkhya Darshan: Yogic Perspective on Theories of Realism.* Munger, Bihar, India: Yoga Publications Trust, 2008.

SCARF: Scottish Archaeological Research Framework. "3.3.1 Burnt Mounds." www.scottishheritagehub.com/content/331-burnt-mounds, accessed September 22, 2017.

Scranton, Laird. *China's Cosmological Prehistory.* Rochester, Vt.: Inner Traditions, 2014.

———. *The Mystery of Skara Brae.* Rochester, Vt.: Inner Traditions, 2016.

———. *Sacred Symbols of the Dogon.* Rochester, Vt.: Inner Traditions, 2007.

Sholom, Gershom. *Origins of the Kabbalah.* Princeton, N.J.: Princeton University Press, 1962.

Shortland, Edward. *Maori Religion and Mythology.* London: Longmans, Green and Co., 1882.

Shrempp, Gregory. *Magical Arrows: The Maori, the Greeks, and Folklore of the Universe.* Madison: University of Wisconsin Press, 1992.

Sutton, Douglas G., ed. *The Origins of the First New Zealanders.* Auckland, New Zealand: Auckland University Press, 1994.

Tregear, Edward. *The Aryan Maori.* Wellington, New Zealand: George Didsbury, Government Printer, 1885.

———. *The Maori-Polynesian Comparative Dictionary.* Wellington, New Zealand: Lyon and Blair, 1891.

———. *The Maori Race.* Wanganui, New Zealand, A. D. Willis, Printer and Publisher, 1904.

Wilson, John. "History—Māori Arrival and Settlement." Te Ara—The Encyclopedia of New Zealand (online). www.TeAra.govt.nz/en/history /page-1.

Index

aakhu, 38, 68

aaru, 50, 102–8, 112–13, 119, 131, 134–35, 138, 140, 153–55, 161–62

adze, 50–51, 78

African, 31, 43, 59, 101, 133, 138–39, 145, 160–61

ahamkara, 100

ahuwera, 106

Akhnaten, 14

albino, 132

Amen, 14, 20, 63, 87

Amma, 20, 46, 63–64, 74, 144–46

ancestor, 16, 21, 29, 32, 34, 48–49, 70, 109–10, 133, 135, 155, 157

Argat, 62, 84, 103–4

ariki ("firstborn priest"), 63, 105, 108, 116, 119, 139, 155

ark, 48, 62–64, 146

arou. See aaru

Arou Priest, 102, 108, 119, 140, 154

Arrow, 69, 148

ascension, 16, 22, 47, 49–50, 56–57, 62–63, 84, 87, 89, 100, 106, 151, 157, 159

astronomy, 108, 116, 118–19, 155, 158, 161

atom, 1, 16, 42–43, 53–54, 64, 69, 92, 142

atua, 38, 99, 129, 131

auau, 85

Australia, 3, 5, 12, 141, 160

awaken, 53, 63, 68, 90, 128–30, 134, 141, 149

axis, 48, 116, 125–27, 153

axis tilt, 125, 127

Bambara, 43

basket, 22, 47–48, 89, 92, 146, 151

baskets, three, 22, 47–48, 89, 151

Bauval, Robert, 13

bell, 53, 70

big bang, 98

bird, 11, 22–23, 50, 90, 123, 136

black hole, 98, 124

breath, 39, 54, 68, 77, 80

Buddha, 12, 53

Buddhist, 2, 6, 12–13, 15, 32, 48, 52–59, 69–71, 88, 99, 103–4, 116, 126, 150, 152, 157

bummo, 85

cairn, 122

Calabi-Yau space, 28, 54–55, 76, 80, 143

Calame-Griaule, Genevieve, 9, 43, 47, 148
canoe, 3–4, 91, 126, 134–35, 140–43
cardinal points, 48, 126, 153
chet/chait, 18
China, 2, 5, 7, 14, 20, 22, 35, 56, 105, 155, 160
circumcision, 32, 132
collarbone, 25–26
commandment, 68, 136
conception, 15–16, 85
Cook, James, 3, 121
cosmogonic egg, 15, 29, 33, 52
creation, Maori phases of, 90–93

dance, 12, 76, 80
departmental gods, 22, 25, 28
destroyer, 23
Dharni Penu, 12, 67, 71–72, 77, 92
Dieterlen, Germaine, 25, 46, 63, 122, 144–45
dimension, 36, 41, 47, 54, 76, 85, 91, 102, 105, 142
Dimly-Seen, 132
DNA, 12, 160
Dongba, 33
Dravidian, 2, 33, 65
druid, 115
duality, 15–16, 28–29, 39, 96–97, 108, 145, 157, 159, 161
dung beetle, 84, 159
dwarf star, 72

Earth Mother, 17, 30, 44, 54, 72–73, 82, 90–92, 125–31, 153, 158, 162
egg, fertilized, 15

egg-in-a-ball, 15, 36, 48
egg-of-the-world, 23, 28–29, 37–38, 41–43, 48, 54, 64, 75, 78–79, 85, 90, 92, 101–2, 104, 124–25, 129, 136, 143, 146
El (deity), 93–94
electron, 79
elephant, 12, 18, 69, 72, 76–77, 79, 92
Elephantine, 6, 12, 71, 160
Elysian, 94, 103, 107–8, 154
embrace, 15–16, 43, 61–62, 67–68, 84, 97–98, 146, 148, 151, 157
enlightenment, 95, 100
entanglement, 79
equinox, 55
esoteric, 1, 6, 10, 14, 20, 22, 24, 33, 45, 59, 65, 81, 89, 95, 120, 157, 161

fairy, 133, 136, 138, 156
fairy mound, 132, 158
Faroe Islands, 50, 104, 108–9, 135–36, 156
Faroese, 2, 113, 116, 134, 156
feast, 136–37
felag ("academy"), 116
feminine energy, 15, 39, 41, 66, 92, 120
Fertile Crescent, 6, 11–12, 52, 65, 71, 152, 159–60
fertility, 61, 73, 97, 152
Field of Reeds/Offerings, 94, 103–5, 107–9, 135, 154, 161–62
filidha ("learned seers"), 115
finger, 41, 60
Firstborn, 63, 105, 119, 155, 161
First Time, 12, 150
First World, 38, 90

force, 27, 42, 51, 63, 82, 89–90, 98, 112, 124, 146

fulacht fiadh (stone structure), 113–16

Ganesha, 12–13, 64, 69, 72, 74–80, 92

gardener, 139

gatekeeper, 79

Genesis, Book of, 20, 67, 90, 92–93, 127, 141, 151

geometry, 41, 48, 55–56, 70, 102, 105

getpetkai, 87

Giza, 13, 56, 88

gnomon, 55, 126

Gobekli Tepe, 2, 6, 11–12, 23, 40–41, 58–63, 71, 88–89, 97, 105–6, 122, 146, 150–53, 160

gravity, 17, 27, 42, 98, 124

Griaule, Marcel, 25, 29, 36–37, 43, 46–47, 63, 74, 81, 92, 122, 132, 144–45, 148–49

hand, 20, 41–42, 60–62, 97, 146, 151

Haumia, 28

Hawaiki, 3, 108, 134, 138

hawk, 23, 50

Hebrew, 2, 18, 23, 32–33, 37, 39, 66, 93, 127, 129, 134, 150–52, 154

hemisphere, 26, 47, 64, 134, 153, 161

herald, 85

Het Pet Ka Yah, 88, 151

hidden, 1, 20, 26, 30, 63, 130

Hindu, 2, 6, 12–13, 23, 53–54, 71–72, 77–78, 89–90, 100, 112, 128–30, 134, 141, 152

Hogon, 32, 95, 120, 122

Hotunui, 135–36

house, 13, 26, 39, 53, 60–61, 68, 84–85, 90, 94, 100, 102, 107, 109, 111, 113, 115, 118, 125, 128–29, 134, 141

House of Life/House of Books, 100, 107, 109, 111

huri ("to twist"), 43, 126

huru ("emission of light"), 37, 43, 90

Icelandic, 2, 94

i ching. See yijing

Io (deity), 19–21, 89, 94, 128

Jubilee Year, 32

Kabbalism, 18, 32, 128, 144–45

khore, 37

kirkja ("house of worship"), 113

light, 16, 22, 28, 38, 43–44, 62, 66–68, 73, 83, 88–94, 116, 126–27, 129, 134, 144, 146, 155

light, speed of, 36

Living Water, 73–74

Lower World, 108, 135, 156

maat ("correct knowledge"), 100

manifestation, 100, 148

masculine energy, 15, 39, 66

mass, 17, 26–28, 36, 42–43, 51, 54–55, 64, 72–73, 78, 80, 85–86, 88, 90, 92, 96, 106, 136, 142–43, 148

mata ("the face" or "observation"), 77, 83, 118, 126–27, 140–43

membrane, 42

mnemonic, 46, 97, 120

Mulberry Tree, 50
multiplicity, 26, 35, 55, 99, 145

Naga, 130, 132, 137
naherangi, 107
Na–Khi, 5, 33, 160
navel, 56–57
Neith, 48, 129, 160
nem, 139
night, 44–45, 86, 93, 117–18, 134
Noah, 83
nonexistence, 16, 37, 49, 84, 100
nummo, 17, 25–26, 110, 133, 137–39, 144, 147–49, 160–61
Nummo Fish, 25–26

obstacle, 69, 76–80, 84
occult, 111–12, 118–20
Ogo, 38, 129, 144–45
Ogotemmeli, 29, 37, 81, 92
orbit, 35
ordinal numbers, 35–36, 38–39, 48
Orion, 13, 17, 23
Orissa, 112
Orkney, 13, 50, 62, 67, 84, 89, 93–94, 101–10, 113–16, 125, 130–31, 133–39, 146–47, 152–58, 160–62
Osiris, 56, 87, 149
overturn, 43, 90, 126–28, 135, 153, 158, 162

paleness, 25, 46, 63, 77, 100, 122, 144–45
Papa, 21–22, 27–29, 49, 62, 98, 110, 125, 134
Papae, 110, 131, 133, 139, 147, 155, 160

per-aa, 104, 135–36
perception, 15–16, 25–26, 28, 36, 38, 67, 83, 85, 97, 130, 141
Peti, 110, 131–39, 147, 155–56, 158, 160
Pharaoh, 14, 31, 104, 116, 135–36, 160
phoneme, 8, 16–18, 36, 38, 40, 42, 52, 54–55, 57, 59, 62, 64, 68, 70, 78–80, 84, 103, 155
phonemes, complex, 17–18, 79
phonemes, symbolic, 16–17
photon, 43
pil/fil, 18, 69, 76–77
pillar, 11, 61–62, 89, 97, 122, 146, 151
pitha, 56
plant, growth of, 28, 40, 50, 54, 102, 122
plateau, 56, 60
po, 1, 43–44, 53–54, 69, 76, 86, 92, 142, 157
po pilu, 36, 38, 41–43, 54–55, 64, 68–69, 76, 92
potbelly, 73
primal parents, 21–22, 28
primordial time, 43, 86
puri, 111–13
pygmy, 132, 137, 139, 147, 158, 160

rainbow, 116
Rangi, 21–22, 27–28, 49, 62, 98, 125–26, 128, 134
reed/reedleaf, 54, 93–94, 103–5, 107–9, 113, 135, 142, 154, 161–62
Rehua (deity), 78–79
reversal, 14, 24, 48, 62, 72–74, 77, 87, 89, 106, 127–28, 131, 151, 153

Rongo, 23–25, 27, 29

Ruaumoko, 29–30, 126–27

Sakti Cult, 2, 6, 12–13, 58, 65, 67, 71–72, 95, 99, 112, 120, 122, 137, 151–52

Samkhya, 95–100

Sanskrit, 2, 32, 52–53, 65–66, 95

Sati, 13, 56, 72, 74, 76–77, 81, 149

School of Reeds, 111–18, 162

Scotland, 6, 13, 67, 84, 93–94, 99, 101, 109–10, 114, 125, 132, 36, 147, 152, 154–58, 160

Scottish-Gaelic, 2

season, 55, 92, 102

Second World, 38, 42–43, 64, 89–90, 112

seed, 28, 43, 49–50, 54, 102

sekhet, 102

Sekhet Aaru ("Field of Reeds"), 103, 105, 108, 154, 161–62

sieve, 54–55, 69, 78

Sirius, 17, 23, 56, 72

Sith, 132

Siva/Shiva, 13–14, 54, 56, 77–78, 87

skaill, 67, 94

Skara Brae, 13, 41, 62, 67, 89–91, 93–94, 101–3, 105, 107, 110, 113, 124–25, 131, 135, 138–39, 141, 147, 153–55, 157–58

sleeping goddess, 53, 68, 90, 92, 107, 128, 130, 134, 141

solstice, 55

space, 16, 27–28, 34, 36, 40–41, 47, 50, 82, 85–86, 88, 91–93, 105, 124–25, 127–28, 141–43, 148, 150, 159

Sphinx, 13, 40, 88

spiral, 23, 29, 43, 64, 76, 101, 104–5, 124, 145–46, 148

square, 25–26, 41, 47–48, 62, 82, 132, 144

standing stone, 11, 56, 73, 102, 122, 150–51, 158

stellar bubble, 124

string theory, 28, 54, 91, 124, 143

stupa, 13, 32, 48, 55–56, 70

sundial, 55

sun glyph, 15

supplication, 8, 122

Tahi ("one"), 38–40

Tamil, 2, 33, 53, 65–71, 75, 152

Tana Penu, 12, 17, 67, 72–73, 77, 92, 131, 151

Tane, 22–24, 27–28, 47–48, 50, 72–74, 89

Tangaroa, 25–27

tapu, 20–21, 59–61, 81, 117, 157

Tasman, Abel, 3

Tawhiri-Matea, 27

te kore ("non-existence"), 35–43, 81

temau/toymu, 23–24, 70, 86

Third World, 38, 43, 89

Tiki, 74

toguna ("discussion house"), 39

tohunga ("expert"), 39, 99, 119–23

tonu, 86

torsion theory, 124

Tree of Life, 50, 74, 83

Tu (deity), 23–24, 70, 77

tua, 38–39, 91, 122, 131–32, 142

tuahu ("sacred spot"), 121–22, 135–37

Tuat, 24, 38, 42, 86, 122
Tuatha de Danaan, 131–32, 137
Turkish, 2, 33, 71, 75
tusk, 64, 76–77, 79
twist, 29, 36, 43, 137

Underworld, 24, 30, 38, 44, 64, 86, 90,
    122, 126–27, 132, 155–57, 161–62
unity, 26, 35, 55, 123, 145, 149
universe, formation of, 15, 33, 44,
    52–53, 73, 83, 93, 98, 115, 129,
    145
universe, material/nonmaterial, 17,
    29, 38–39, 41, 50, 56–57, 59, 66,
    82–84, 88, 98, 100, 128, 144–46,
    148–49
universes, fourteen, 41, 74, 91, 142,
    144

Vedic, 2, 6, 12, 71, 152
vibration, 16–17, 27, 39–40, 43, 54,
    68, 79, 85, 90, 102, 142–43
Vishnu, 112, 130, 137
vortex, 43, 55, 91–92, 124
Vulture Peak, 59, 150

wananga ("occult knowledge"),
    111–12, 128
weaving, 12, 31, 37, 49, 78
whaka ("to cause"), 59, 68, 117,
    129–30
Wharekura ("School of Reeds"),
    108–9, 111–18
Whiro, 28–29, 127
wind, 27, 49, 51, 54, 68, 76, 85, 99, 103,
    105, 107–8, 135–36, 142
wizard, 120
womb, 40, 92, 135
written language, 14, 16, 32, 45

Yah, 66–68, 83, 88–90, 92–94, 127,
    129, 133, 150–54
yala, 66, 85
year, 2–4, 6–7, 32, 46, 55, 63, 92, 102,
    104, 114, 116–17, 131, 137, 145,
    157–58
yijing, 17, 35
yoga, 95
Yogini, 95, 120

Zep Tepi, 12, 59